Rousseau's State of Nature

ROUSSEAU'S
STATE OF NATURE

AN INTERPRETATION
OF THE
DISCOURSE ON INEQUALITY

MARC F. PLATTNER

Northern Illinois University Press

DeKalb / 1979

Publication of this book was made possible
by a grant from the Earhart Foundation.

We wish to thank St. Martin's Press for permission to quote passages
in Judith R. and Roger D. Masters's translation of *Jean-Jacques
Rousseau: The First and Second Discourses*, © 1964. Reprinted by
permission of St. Martin's Press, Inc., New York, N.Y.

Library of Congress Cataloging in Publication Data

Plattner, Marc F   1945–
  Rousseau's state of nature.

  Includes bibliographical references and index.
    1. Rousseau, Jean Jacques, 1712–1788–Political
science. 2. Rousseau, Jean Jacques, 1712–1778.
Discourse sur l'origine et les fondements de l'iné-
galité parmi les hommes. I. Title.
JC179.R9P57   320.1′1   78–60453
ISBN 0–87580–074–2

To Jacqueline Stark

CONTENTS

PREFACE

THIS STUDY IS DEVOTED to the interpretation of a single book, the *Discourse on Inequality* of Jean-Jacques Rousseau. Moreover, it does not even pretend to be an exhaustive commentary upon that work. Instead, it focuses upon a single aspect of the *Discourse on Inequality*—Rousseau's concept of the state of nature. I have chosen this approach because I believe that Rousseau's teaching about the state of nature lies at the very heart of his entire theoretical enterprise, and that a careful interpretation of this teaching is an indispensable first step toward understanding the seemingly most contradictory elements of his thought. It is for the readers of this study to decide to what extent these claims are justified.

Whatever merit this volume contains can be attributed primarily to the education that I received from Allan Bloom. It was he who first introduced me to political philosophy and to Rousseau when I was a freshman at Yale University; and during my graduate school days at Cornell University, it was he who supervised the doctoral dissertation that eventually culminated in this book. While at Cornell I also had the extraordinary good fortune of encountering four other outstanding teachers—Werner Dannhauser, Walter Berns, Myron Rush, and Richard Kennington.

An invaluable contribution to my work was made by my wife Jacqui, to whom this book is dedicated. I am also most grateful to my parents, whose exhortations, though not always welcome when they were made, helped to spur me on through some dark hours. Without Irving Kristol's characteristically generous encouragement and advice, this book might never have been completed. I also wish to thank my friend James H. Nichols, Jr., for his valuable suggestions about revising certain points in the text. Finally, I am especially grateful to the Earhart Foundation for its generous financial assistance.

I have not heavily relied on the work of modern commentators on Rousseau, with one important exception: the chapter on Rousseau in Leo Strauss's *Natural Right and History* (Chicago: University of Chicago Press, 1957). This compact but brilliant essay decisively influenced my thinking about Rousseau.

All citations to the works of Rousseau are keyed to the Pléiade edition: *Oeuvres Complètes de Jean-Jacques Rousseau*, 4 vols. (Paris: Bibliothèque de la Pléiade, 1959–69). In the footnotes this edition is designated as P. In the case of Rousseau's *Discourse on the Sciences and Arts* and *Discourse on Inequality*, citations are first made to Roger D. Masters, ed., *Jean-Jacques Rousseau: The First and Second Discourses*, trans. Roger D. and Judith R. Masters (New York: St. Martin's Press, 1964), with corresponding page references in the Pléiade edition added in brackets. Quotations from the two *Discourses* are drawn from the Masters edition; in the few instances where I have departed from their generally excellent translation, the French words in question are provided in parentheses. All translations of other works of Rousseau and of other authors (except where indicated) are my own.

Marc F. Plattner
New York, New York

Rousseau's State of Nature

1

Introduction

JEAN-JACQUES ROUSSEAU was the first great *modern* critic of bourgeois society. He did not attack the emergent bourgeois order in the name of aristocracy or of the Church; none of the *philosophes* with whom he quarreled was more firmly opposed to the principles of feudalism than was Rousseau himself. Instead, he opposed bourgeois society in the name of the very principles to which it itself appealed—freedom and equality. Rousseau was the first political philosopher to attack bourgeois society from the Left.

Indeed, Rousseau was the first writer to give the term "bourgeois" the kind of pejorative connotation that it often conveys today. In his *Emile* he presents the following description:

> Always in contradiction with himself, always floating between his desires and his duties, he will never be either man or citizen; he will be good neither for himself nor for others. This will be one of the men of our age: a Frenchman, an Englishman, a *bourgeois*; this will be nothing.[1]

[*3*]

As this passage makes clear, Rousseau uses the term "bourgeois" not to distinguish a particular socioeconomic class but rather to denominate a cetain kind of human being. The bourgeois is opposed to "man" on the one hand, and to the "citizen" on the other. He lacks the naturalness and independence of the genuine individual, who always follows his own desires; and he lacks the public-spiritedness and selflessness of the genuine citizen, who always fulfills his duties. He therefore is "good neither for himself nor for others."

This attack on the men of his own time from the two very different perspectives of the genuine individual and the good citizen is characteristic of Rousseau's thought as a whole. It is this ambivalence that has given rise to the lengthy and still unresolved debate among students of Rousseau as to whether he is an "individualist" or a "collectivist." Whichever side one may take in this debate, it should be recognized that the co-presence of these opposite tendencies is not simply the result of some idiosyncrasy of Rousseau's personality or some peculiar confusion of his thought. For this same ambivalence between individualism and collectivism has been a persistent feature of much subsequent social and political criticism, and has emerged in a particularly striking fashion in the left-wing thought of the present era.

Thus the bourgeoisie (in the United States, one usually says "the middle class") is often simultaneously accused by contemporary radicals of slavish conformity and of rampant selfishness. There is, of course, no necessary contradiction in this two-fold accusation (which exactly parallels Rousseau's own critique). But the positive implications of these two criticisms point in opposite directions. The assault on conformity presupposes a high regard for individualism, while the attack on selfishness presupposes a high regard for community. And the requirements of individualism and those of community must often come into conflict. Yet very few of those who attack bourgeois society are willing wholly to abandon either of these standards in the name of the other. Thus it has not been uncommon, for example, to find a critic who in one breath demands the most extreme freedom for the individual writer or artist against any interference by the political community, and in the next breath expresses his admiration for a regime (like the People's Republic of China or Castro's Cuba) that openly imposes the most severe restrictions on the freedom of its own writers and artists.

It would, of course, be unrealistic to expect a rigorous consistency of thought to inform most social and political criticism. Yet the persistence and prevalence of the particular inconsistency identified here indicates that it is due to more than just sloppy thinking. Perhaps there may be a hidden root from which these two linked but opposing tendencies on the part of critics of bourgeois society spring. This suspicion is reinforced by the fact that in the thought of a single philosopher, Jean-Jacques Rousseau, there emerged both a more extreme individualism and a more extreme collectivism than any previous political philosopher had proposed.[2] There is reason to believe that an investigation of the theoretical foundations of Rousseau's political philosophy may shed some light on the common premises that underlie both modern individualism and modern collectivism.

The Discourse on the Sciences and Arts

All the essential elements of Rousseau's indictment of bourgeois society are contained in his first two principal writings, the *Discourse on the Sciences and Arts* (or *First Discourse*), published in 1750, and the *Discourse on the Origin and Foundations of Inequality Among Men* (or *Second Discourse*), published in 1755. These two works are especially severe in their condemnation of the commercial spirit of modernity, and they share many other common themes in their criticism of the so-

[5]

ciety in which Rousseau lived. Yet in other respects the *First Discourse* and the *Second Discourse* appear to express very different orientations. In terms of the dichotomy outlined above, the *First Discourse* chiefly represents the collectivist side of Rousseau's thought, and the *Second Discourse* the individualist side. The *First Discourse* condemns the cultivation of the arts and sciences as being inimical to the requirements of a good society. Its argument is presented primarily from the standpoint of the citizen. The *Second Discourse*, on the other hand, takes as its model the solitary individual, and it seems to cast doubt upon the worth of any and all political societies.

Yet the contrast between these two works is not as straightforward as it initially appears. First of all, there are important individualist elements present in the *First Discourse*, despite its predominantly collectivist emphasis. In fact, near the very beginning of this work, there appears the following passage:

> While government and laws provide for the safety and well-being of assembled men, the sciences, letters, and arts, less despotic and perhaps more powerful, spread garlands of flowers over the iron chains with which men are burdened, stifle in them that sense of individual liberty for which they seemed to have been born, make them love their slavery, and turn them into what is called civilized peoples.[3]

Here Rousseau appears to identify government and laws (which is to say, political society as such) with chains, despotism, and even slavery, and implicitly to condemn them in the name of "original liberty." This line of argument is further reflected in two important footnotes that praise the freedom and naturalness of the savages of North America.[4] In a similar vein, Rousseau deplores the uniformity that prevails in the *moeurs* of his contemporaries, and complains that in "this herd called society" men follow established usages rather than their own inclinations (*génie*).[5]

As has been noted, however, the principal thrust of the

[6]

First Discourse moves in a very different direction. Rather than urging men to follow their inclinations, it calls on them to fulfill their duties. Rather than upholding as a model the independence of the savage, it exalts the public-spiritedness of noble Romans like Fabricius and Cato the Censor. And far from condemning all governments and laws, it lavishes the highest praise on political societies like Sparta and early Republican Rome that exercised the strictest control over the private lives of their citizens.

The key word in the *First Discourse* is "virtue." At the beginning of the work Rousseau characterizes his intention by stating, "I am not abusing science . . . I am defending virtue before virtuous men."[6] Rousseau attacks the arts and sciences not in themselves, but insofar as they are in conflict with virtue. The meaning that is given to the term "virtue" in the *First Discourse* is sometimes ambiguous, but one can safely say that it is identified principally with the morality of the citizen, and that it consists in the performance of one's duties.

In contending that the cultivation of the arts and sciences tends to corrupt morals, Rousseau must deal with two somewhat different questions: (1) What is the fate of virtue in a society that fosters the arts and sciences? and (2) Does virtue depend upon science or knowledge? Rousseau's answer to the first of these questions is most clearly understood in terms of the contrast that he sets up between virtues and talents. In a society where the arts and sciences are cultivated, talents will come to be esteemed and rewarded, and virtue will be correspondingly neglected. This argument is particularly applicable to the principles of bourgeois society. The capitalist system is unambiguously intended to reward the able, the clever, and the industrious; at best, it is in itself perfectly indifferent to the virtues of the citizen. Thomas Hobbes, in many respects the quintessential bourgeois philosopher, had asserted that "the *value,* or Worth of a man, is as of all other things, his

[7]

price."[7] It is in response to this view of man and to the kind of society to which it gives rise that Rousseau protests: "What will become of virtue when one must get rich at any price?"[8] Rousseau's conclusion that societies that honor the arts and sciences are likely to undervalue the virtues of the citizen is unequivocal.

The second of the questions referred to above is much less apparent at the surface of the *First Discourse*, but it too must be answered in order to give a complete account of the relationship between science and morality. Rousseau praises the practice of virtue rather than the study of virtue, and devotion to one's duties rather than devotion to the sciences. But these very formulations raise the question of how one knows what virtue is and what duties one should perform. The wholehearted condemnation of the arts and sciences in the name of morality would be possible only if the knowledge of their true duties were available to men independently of science or philosophy.

Rousseau's position on *this* question is exceedingly equivocal. The First Part of the *Discourse* begins as follows:

It is a grand and beautiful sight to see man emerge from obscurity somehow by his own efforts; dissipate, by the light of his reason, the darkness in which nature has enveloped him; rise above himself; soar intellectually into celestial regions; traverse with giant steps, like the sun, the vastness of the universe; and—what is even grander and more difficult —*come back to himself (rentrer en soi) to study man and know his nature, his duties, and his end.*[9]

Though this passage is open to varying interpretations, it at least seems to suggest that knowledge of the most theoretical kind (i.e., of the "celestial regions") is the necessary foundation of knowledge of man and his duties. This same view would also seem to underlie Rousseau's plea later in the *First Discourse* that great scientists like Bacon, Descartes, and Newton (whom he calls "preceptors of the human race") should be made the

[8]

advisers of princes, and should help to instruct peoples in their duties.[10] It might be argued that since this suggestion is confined largely to a monarchical context—and since Rousseau clearly indicates his preference for republicanism—its importance can be minimized. Yet even in a purely republican context, the question of how the citizens learn their duties cannot be avoided. This problem is nicely posed in Rousseau's reference to Sparta as "that city as renowned for its happy *ignorance* as for the *wisdom* of its laws."[11] Indeed, it might be said that Spartan ignorance is happy precisely because of the wisdom of Spartan laws. But what is the source of the wisdom that produces good laws? Must not the wisdom of the legislator presuppose some kind of knowledge that goes beyond the knowledge of the ordinary law-abiding citizen? In the preface to his comedy *Narcisse*, Rousseau claims that in the *First Discourse* he has "brought to light something very consoling and very useful in showing that all these vices [i.e., of modern society] do not belong so much to man, *as to man badly governed*."[12] He thus seems to imply that he teaches a kind of political science that might be employed by legislators or rulers to make men more virtuous.

Yet these occasional indications that virtue might after all in some way be in need of science (whether theoretical science or some kind of autonomous political or legislative science) are overshadowed in the *First Discourse* by statements implying or asserting the contrary. In particular, the famous concluding paragraph of the work gives the strongest possible expression of the absolute independence of virtue, and the immediate availability of moral knowledge to all men:

O virtue! Sublime science of simple souls, are so many difficulties and preparations needed to know you? Are not your principles engraved in all hearts, and is it not enough in order to learn your laws to commune with oneself (*rentrer en soi-même*) and listen to the voice of one's conscience in the silence of the passions. That is true philosophy (*la véritable philosophie*), let us know how to be satisfied with it. . . ."[13]

Here, in appealing to the "sublime science of simple souls" and "true philosophy," which have their locus in the conscience rather than in the understanding, Rousseau devotes his final words to affirming that morality has no need of science or philosophy in the usual sense of those terms.

The Discourse on Inequality

In the light of this emphatic conclusion to the *First Discourse*, it is rather striking to note that Rousseau's next major work, the *Discourse on the Origin and Foundations of Inequality Among Men*, immediately reveals itself as a philosophic or scientific book. The very first sentence of the Preface reads: "The most useful and least advanced of all human knowledge seems to me to be that of man";[14] and appended to this sentence is a note that quotes a passage from the *Natural History* of Buffon, preceded by the following remark of Rousseau: "From the outset I rely with confidence on one of those authorities that are respectable for philosophers because they come from a solid and sublime reason, which philosophers alone know how to find and appreciate."[15] Thus at the very beginning of the *Second Discourse* Rousseau both identifies himself as a philosopher and affirms the worth and nobility of theory.

In the *First Discourse* Rousseau had depicted himself as "an honorable man who knows nothing," and had characterized the question that he addressed as one concerned not with "metaphysical subtleties," but with the "happiness of mankind."[16] He refers to the subject of the *Second Discourse* as "one of the most interesting questions that philosophy might propose, and unhappily for us, one of the thorniest that philosophers might resolve."[17] In the *First Discourse* Rousseau presents himself as an "orator" who is speaking in *defense* of virtue.[18] The language that he uses in speaking of his relationship to his judges is reminiscent of the language of the courtroom. He appeals to them as virtuous men rather than as learned men. In the *Second Discourse*, by contrast, Rousseau "imagines" himself "in the Lyceum of Athens . . . with Plato and Xenocrates for judges. . . ."[19]

In the *First Discourse*, where Rousseau speaks primarily as a moral man, the key word, to repeat, is "virtue." In the *Second Discourse*, where Rousseau speaks primarily as a philosopher or scientist, the key word is "nature." And the focus on nature brings to the fore the individualist side of Rousseau's thought that remained largely submerged in the *First Discourse*. In the cold light of science, the claims of morality and citizenship—which override all other claims in the earlier work—are called into question. The *Second Discourse* points to the kinship between science and individualism, just as the *First Discourse* had brought out the kinship between morality and community.

The scientific investigation that Rousseau undertakes in the *Second Discourse* consists chiefly in an examination of the "state of nature," or that condition of mankind which is characterized by the absence of any sort of community whatever. And this study of the state of nature leads to a radical critique of civil society itself and all its most essential institutions: the family, private property, and the laws. The social criticism of the *Second Discourse* is aimed at the genuine citizen as well as the bourgeois:

> . . . the citizen, always active, sweats, agitates himself, torments himself incessantly in order to seek still more laborious occupations; he works to death, he even rushes to it in order to get in condition to live, or renounces life in order to acquire immortality. He pays court to the great whom he hates, and to the rich whom he scorns. He spares nothing in order to obtain the honor of serving them; he proudly boasts of his

baseness and their protection; and proud of his slavery, he speaks with disdain of those who do not have the honor of sharing it.[20]

The counterpoint to Rousseau's attack on civil man is his praise of the savage. The superiority of the savage's way of life, as Rousseau presents it, consists above all in its greater freedom. "Freedom" or "liberty" (in either case, the French "*liberté*") is perhaps as important a word in the *Second Discourse* as is "nature." Indeed, freedom and nature belong together, for freedom is an "essential gift of nature."[21] The freedom of the savage lies in an almost total *independence* of all other men, and the consequent license to act however he wishes and always to follow his own inclinations. In the name of this absolute freedom and of nature, Rousseau praises the most primitive men—men who have "no known duties" and are utterly lacking in morality or virtue.

Yet this is not the whole story in the *Second Discourse*. For alongside the extreme individualism that seems to dominate this work, there is significant evidence of that aspect of Rousseau's thought which takes the side of community and of citizenship. This is apparent, for example, in a few scattered references to Sparta, which is treated no less favorably in the *Second Discourse* than it was in the *First Discourse*.[22] More striking still is the "Dedication to the Republic of Geneva" that precedes the text of the *Second Discourse*. In this Dedication Rousseau bestows the highest praise upon his homeland, and emphasizes in particular those aspects of the Genevan polity that resemble the ancient republics praised in the *First Discourse*. That is to say, Geneva is extolled because, as a truly close-knit community, it imposes severe moral and legal restraints upon the lives of its citizens—constraints that place narrow limits on the highly individualistic freedom generally favored in the rest of the *Second Discourse*. Moreover, in the Dedication Rousseau carefully distinguishes freedom "from an unbridled license which is its opposite," and states, "I would have wished to live and die free, that is to say so subject to the laws that neither I nor anyone else could shake off their honorable yoke."²³ This conception of freedom as perfect obedience to the laws is clearly very different from the individualistic conception of freedom that informs Rousseau's praise of the savage.

The "Dedication to the Republic of Geneva" and Rousseau's affirmation of a notion of freedom fully compatible with the demands of community indicate that, despite its radical individualism, the *Second Discourse* is not animated by a simply antipolitical point of view. And indeed, in the Preface Rousseau makes it clear that this work is actually guided by a political intention. In the first place, he states that the kind of inquiry that he will make into the natural state of man is necessary for arriving at a true conception of natural right or natural law: ". . . so long as we do not know natural man, we would try in vain to determine the law he has received or that which best suits his constitution."²⁴ It is true, however, that Rousseau never provides a clear statement of such a natural law; hence one might argue that the understanding of natural law or right to which his inquiry leads imposes no limitations on the unbounded freedom he attributes to natural man, and therefore is incapable of supplying any basis for human community.

But whatever the merit of such an argument, and whatever the status of natural law in Rousseau's thought, there can be no question that he believes his analysis of the state of nature is indispensable for attaining knowledge of the proper or legitimate ordering of political society. "This same study of original man," he asserts, ". . . is also the only good means one could use to remove those crowds of difficulties which present themselves concerning the origin of moral inequality, *the true foundations of the body politic, the reciprocal rights of its members*, and a thousand similar questions as important as they are ill explained."[25] And in the Second Part of the *Second Discourse*, Rousseau begins to set forth, albeit in an admittedly provisional manner, the insights into the "true foundations of the body politic" that have been prepared by his study of the state of nature. These preliminary reflections are later given a developed and definitive presentation in the *Social Contract*, Rousseau's most famous and most clearly political writing.

It is the *Social Contract* that tends to be the prime evidence of those who view Rousseau as a collectivist. And yet the *Social Contract* plainly reveals its dependence on the state of nature set forth in the *Second Discourse*.[26] Rousseau's teaching about the state of nature thus appears to be at the same time the source of his most extreme individualism and the crucial underpinning of his most extreme collectivism. It may be expected, therefore, that an examination of the state of nature as it is presented in the *Second Discourse* will help to uncover the theoretical roots of the tension between individualism and collectivism in Rousseau's thought as a whole.

Notes

[1] *Emile*, P, 4:249–50 (italics mine).

[2] In characterizing one tendency in Rousseau's thought as "collectivism," I do not necessarily mean to convey any connotation either of authoritarianism or of socialism. This term—for want of a better—is used simply to designate that point of view which regards the individual merely as a part (or fraction) of that greater whole constituted by the political community.

[3] *First Discourse*, p. 36 [P, 3:7–8].

[4] Ibid., pp. 36, 42 [P, 3:7, 11–12].

[5] Ibid., p. 38 [P, 3:8].

[6] Ibid., p. 34 [P, 3:6].

[7] Thomas Hobbes, *Leviathan*, ed. Michael Oakeshott (Oxford: Basil Blackwell, 1960), 1, chap. 10, p. 57.

[8] *First Discourse*, p. 51 [P, 3:19].

[9] Ibid., p. 35 [P, 3:6] (italics mine).

[10] Ibid., pp. 63–64 [P, 3:29–30].

[11] Ibid., p. 43 [P, 3:12] (italics mine).

[12] *Narcisse*, P, 2:969 (italics mine).

[13] *First Discourse*, p. 64 [P, 3:30].

[14] *Second Discourse*, p. 91 [P, 3:122].

[15] Ibid., Note B, p. 182 [P, 3:195].

[16] *First Discourse*, pp. 33, 34 [P, 3:5, 3].

[17] *Second Discourse*, p. 91 [P, 3:122].

[18] *First Discourse*, p. 34 [P, 3:5].

[19] *Second Discourse*, p. 103 [P, 3:133].

[20] Ibid., p. 179 [P, 3:192].

[21] Ibid., p. 168 [P, 3:184].

[22] Ibid., pp. 89, 106, 163, 173 [P, 3:119, 135, 180, 187–88].

[23] Ibid., pp. 79, 80 [P, 3:112, 113].

[24] Ibid., p. 95 [P, 3:125].

[25] Ibid., p. 96 [P, 3:126] (italics mine).

[26] This emerges most clearly in Book 1, chapter 8, of the *Social Contract*.

2

The Historical Status of the State of Nature

THERE IS CONSIDERABLE CONTROVERSY among students of Rousseau about the historical status of the "state of nature" portrayed in the *Second Discourse*. Some believe that Rousseau intended to paint as accurate as possible a picture of the historical conditions of the first men[1]; others hold that Rousseau's state of nature was meant to be a purely hypothetical or suppositional construct, whose relation to the actual historical situation of the first men is utterly irrelevant.[2] Both sides in this debate find ample evidence for their interpretations in explicit statements to be found in the *Second Discourse* itself. Hence a third group of scholars has been led to conclude that Rousseau was simply confused or undecided upon this point.[3] Those who believe Rousseau's state of nature is meant to aim at a genuinely historical and factual account can point to the scientific spirit that animated so many eighteenth century thinkers (among them close friends or associates of Rousseau like Diderot, Condillac, and Buffon), and especially to their scientific concern with the origins of man.[4] Those who view the doctrine as purely hypothetical can point to the clearly hypothetical and nonhistorical character of the state of nature in the writings of Pufendorf and the academic natural right theorists of Rousseau's own time.

As the interpretation of this question is of fundamental importance for understanding the *Second Discourse*, it is worthwhile to consider it at length. The *Second Discourse* presents a history of the human race.[5] The reader would naturally be led to conclude that this history is intended to render as accurately as possible what actually happened—except for certain explicit statements by Rousseau seemingly disavowing such an intention and emphasizing the purely hypothetical character of the work. It is necessary, then, to examine these statements with some care. The first and one of the most striking occurs early in the Preface where, clearly referring to the state of nature, Rousseau asserts that "it is no light undertaking to separate what is original from what is artificial in the present nature of man, and to know correctly *a state which no longer exists, which perhaps never existed, which probably never will exist,* and about which it is nevertheless necessary to have a precise notion in order to judge our present state correctly."[6] In a longer passage in the introductory section[7] of the *Discourse* proper, he reveals the grounds for this seemingly paradoxical statement in the Preface:

It did not even enter the minds of most of our philosophers to doubt that the state of nature had existed, even though it is evident from reading the Holy Scriptures that the first man, having received enlightenment and precepts directly from God, was not himself in that state; and that giving the writings of Moses the credence that any Christian philosopher owes them, it must be denied that even before the flood men were ever in the pure state of nature, unless they fell back into it because of some extraordinary event: a paradox that is very embarrassing to defend and altogether impossible to prove.

Let us therefore begin by setting all the facts aside, for they do not affect the question. The researches which can be undertaken concerning this subject must not be taken for historical truths, but only for hypothetical and conditional reasonings better suited to clarify the nature of things than to show their true origin, like those our physicists make every day concerning the formation of the world. Religion commands us to believe that since God Himself took men out of the state of nature immediately after the creation, they are unequal because He wanted them to be so; but it does not forbid us to form conjectures, drawn solely from the nature of man and the beings surrounding him, about what the human race might have become if it had remained abandoned to itself. That is what I am asked, and what I propose to examine in this Discourse.[8]

This passage shows that, whatever his real views on the subject may have been, Rousseau had a powerful motive for presenting his state of nature doctrine as purely hypothetical —namely, the conflict with the authoritative theological teaching in which he otherwise would have found himself. If Rousseau had openly admitted that his state of nature was meant to be historical, he would have in effect been declaring his disbelief in the Biblical account. The dangers that were incurred in crossing the ecclesiastical authorities in matters pertaining to Christian doctrine are only too clear from the hardships and persecutions which the later publication of the *Emile* and the *Social Contract* brought down upon Rousseau himself.[9] And the sensitivity of the particular issues that the *Second Discourse* raised is strikingly demonstrated by the case of the Abbé de Prades, which had caused a considerable stir in Paris only a few years before the publication of the *Second Discourse.*[10]

Furthermore, the subterfuge employed by many eighteenth-century French thinkers of making formal declarations of belief in and obedience to Christian dogma—declarations which are denied by the overall tendency of their writings—

has been recognized by many modern scholars. This practice is particularly conspicuous in the writings of Diderot, Rousseau's closest friend during the period in which the *Second Discourse* was composed. Consider the following statements written by two distinguished scholars of eighteenth-century French thought. The first is by Jean Morel:

> Such boldness of thought exposed its authors to the rancor of the Church. These researches on the origin and development of things, of beings, and of societies were in opposition to the story of Genesis and to the whole Bible. His *Interpretation of Nature* would have landed Diderot in the Bastille, if it had not been enveloped in obscurity. But one freed oneself from the dogma by means of verbal concessions; one made a display of respect for the theological verities, and the bold idea was presented as a hypothesis. A tacit convention between the reader and the author put things back into focus (*remettait les choses au point*), and the excess of submission indicated precisely what was novel in the thought. It is a misinterpretation (*un contre sens*) to take these declarations literally.[11]

The second statement, by George Havens, traces the use of this technique back as far as Descartes:

> Thus the Encyclopedist [i.e., Diderot] probably urged the Citizen of Geneva [i.e., Rousseau] towards boldness, a dangerous boldness of content . . . but probably also showed him how, likes Descartes, like Buffon in his recent *Histoire naturelle*, like Diderot himself in his *Pensées sur l'interpretation de la nature*, Rousseau could limit himself to safer hypotheses and conjectures in detailing the unorthodox history of early humanity, how he could [in the words of Voltaire's maxim] "strike and hide his hand."[12]

Both Morel and Havens flatly conclude that Jean-Jacques Rousseau also employed this manner of writing, and a number of other modern scholars have taken this same view.[13] Further-more, there is, in Rousseau's case, an additional reason to be skeptical about such affirmations of "respect for the theolog-ical verities"—namely, the boldly explicit critique of revelation that he puts in the mouth of his Savoyard Vicar in the *Emile* (and that led to his own subsequent persecution).[14]

These general considerations can be supported by specific evidence in the *Second Discourse* itself that contradicts Rous-seau's pretended obedience to the divinely revealed teaching. In the passage from the Introduction quoted above, Rous-seau speaks of the credence that any "Christian philosopher" owes to the "writings of Moses." Immediately after that long passage, Rousseau continues:

> As my subject concerns man in general, I shall try to use a language that suits all nations, or rather, forgetting times and places in order to think only of the men to whom I speak, I shall imagine myself in the Lyceum of Athens, repeating the lessons of my masters, with Plato and Xenocrates for judges, and the human race for an audience.
>
> O man, whatever country you may come from, whatever your opinions may be, listen: here is your history as I be-lieved it to read, not in the books of your fellowmen, which are liars, but in nature, which never lies. Everything that comes from nature will be true; there will be nothing false except what I have involuntarily put in of my own.[15]

First, it is to be observed that in placing himself in the Lyceum of Athens and forgetting times and places, Rousseau seems to free himself from the duties imposed upon a Christian philosopher.[16] Furthermore, having just referred to the Old Testament as the writings of Moses, he now says that the books of human beings are liars, whereas nature never lies.[17] Finally, in the passage quoted earlier he called for the setting aside of all the facts, saying they were irrelevant to the question at hand; yet at the end of the First Part of the *Discourse* he speaks of "two *facts* given as real" in a context that clearly implies the state of nature is one of these facts.[18]

Now it is time to reconsider Rousseau's statement in the Preface that the state of nature might never have existed at all.[19] That assertion precedes the following passage:

> He who would try to determine exactly what precautions to take in order to make solid observations on this subject would need even more philosophy than is generally thought; and a good solution of the following problem would not seem to me unworthy of the Aristotles and Plinys of our century: *What experiments would be necessary to achieve knowledge of natural man? And what are the means of making these experiments in the midst of society?*[20]

This call for scientific experimentation to determine the characteristics of original man is hardly in accord with a purely hypothetical state of nature that never existed. This same discrepancy is sharpened by the decidedly scientific character of the *Second Discourse* as a whole.[21] Rousseau indicates in several places that his description of the state of nature aims at the character of physics. Thus he criticizes Locke's argument for the naturalness of the family on the grounds that "moral proofs do not have great force in matters of physics."[22] And in the Introduction he compares the "hypothetical and conditional" character of his "researches," not to the hypotheses about the state of nature made by the jurists, but to those "our physicists make . . . concerning the formation of the world."[23] Moreover, he draws heavily upon Buffon's *Natural History*, his own observations of nature, and the ethnographic literature of his time. As Jean Morel has well stated,

> There is certainly a marked tendency toward observation (*l'experience*) on Rousseau's part, a search for scientific facts. The *Discourse* is less syllogistic (*logique*), less a priori than all the treatises that preceded it. It is not a novel. It is

not an epic poem. Rousseau intended, utilizing the means that the science of his epoch provided, *to write the real history of human societies.*[24]

But the most telling indication that Rousseau understands the state of nature as a historical fact is to be found tucked away in Note J, the central and longest note of the *Discourse*. Before proceeding to an analysis of this note, it may be helpful to say a few words more about Rousseau's manner of writing. In a brief "Notice on the Notes" immediately following the Preface, Rousseau seemingly belittles their importance and their relevance to the text proper, and concludes: "Those who have the courage to begin again will be able to amuse themselves a second time in beating the bushes, and try to go through the Notes. There will be little harm if others do not read them at all."[25] As a close analysis of the *Second Discourse* reveals, however, the Notes are essential for understanding a number of the boldest and most crucial elements of Rousseau's teaching. His apparent downgrading of their importance must therefore be viewed in the context of the distinction he draws between two different kinds of readers—those more thorough readers who have the "courage" to read through the Notes, and the "others," who might just as well skip them.[26]

Rousseau draws a similar distinction between two groups of readers in the passage that concludes the First Part of the *Discourse*. There he indicates that he has offered certain "objects to the consideration of [his] judges," while arranging things "so that vulgar readers would have no need to consider them."[27] This passage should in turn be compared with Rousseau's assertion in the Introduction that he imagines himself writing "with Plato and Xenocrates for judges and the human race for an audience."[28] Rousseau may wish to address those philosophers who are his true judges, but his writings will be available to the whole human race, and thus his audience will be comprised primarily of vulgar readers. In his *First Discourse*,

Rousseau had argued that the sciences are harmful and corrupting for the people (*"les hommes vulgaires"*), and that therefore they should be the exclusive preserve of the few great geniuses who are naturally suited to study them.[29] In the *Second Discourse*, in a similar spirit, he regrets the passing of "those happy times when the people did not dabble in philosophy."[30] So if Rousseau wishes to speak to the few, without corrupting the people at large, he must adopt a mode of writing that conceals from vulgar readers knowledge that would be harmful to them.[31]

The character of such a mode of writing has been beautifully described by the British author Samuel Butler, in his interpretation of the work of one of Rousseau's greatest contemporaries, the *Natural History* of Buffon:

> I am inclined to think that a vein of irony pervades the whole, or much the greater part of Buffon's work, and that he intended to convey, one meaning to one set of readers, and another to another; indeed, it is often impossible to believe that he is not writing between his lines for the discerning, what the undiscerning were not intended to see. It must be remembered that his *Natural History* has two sides,—a scientific and a popular one. May we not imagine that Buffon would be unwilling to debar himself from speaking to those who could understand him, and yet would wish like Handel and Shakespeare to address the many, as well as the few? But the only manner in which these seemingly irreconcilable ends could be attained, would be by the use of language which should be self-adjusting to the capacity of the reader.... He would help those who could see to see still further, but he would not dazzle eyes that were yet imperfect with a light brighter than they could stand.[32]

This description would equally well apply to the manner of writing practiced by Rousseau, and one of the tactics Rousseau employed in this enterprise was to "hide" some of his more explosive speculations in the obscure reaches of the Notes.[33] Thus in Note J he speculates upon the possibility that certain animals resembling men, although believed to be beasts by the voyagers who observed them, may really be "true savage men whose race, dispersed in the woods in ancient times . . . was still found in the primitive state of nature."[34] And it is in this context that he makes the only suggestion in the *Discourse* of a specific "experiment" for arriving at knowledge of natural man: He delicately alludes to the mating of a human being and an orangutan for the purpose of seeing whether such a mating would produce fertile offspring. If such a union did produce fertile offspring, this would "verify the *fact*" that the orangutan was really a man in his primitive state.[35] (Rousseau never mentions the possibility that if orangutans really were men, they would be men who had *degenerated* from their natural condition. Such an interpretation, which might reconcile even the proof that orangutans are part of the human species with the Biblical account of man's divine origin, is suggested by a contemporary critic of Rousseau's *Second Discourse*, Jean de Castillon: "If these beings [orangutans] are men, they are not in their primitive state. They have degenerated."[36]) Rousseau's unqualified assertion that even in his own time there might be men still living in the primitive state of nature affords decisive evidence for the interpretation that he regarded the state of nature described in the *Second Discourse* as approximating a factual, historical account.

Notes

¹ See George R. Havens, "Diderot, Rousseau, and the *Discours sur L'Inégalité*," in Otis Fellows and Gita May, eds., *Diderot Studies* (Geneva: Librarie Droz, 1961), 3:260–61; Arthur O. Lovejoy, "The Supposed Primitivism of Rousseau's *Discourse on Inequality*," in Lovejoy's *Essays in the History of Ideas* (Baltimore: Johns Hopkins University Press, 1948), p. 18 (note 4); Roger D. Masters, *The Political Philosophy of Rousseau* (Princeton: Princeton University Press, 1968), pp. 117–18, 198–99; Jean Morel, "Recherches sur les sources du discours de l'inégalité," *Annales de la Société Jean-Jacques Rousseau* (Geneva: A Jullien, 1909), 5:131–38, 198; Leo Strauss, *Natural Right and History* (Chicago: University of Chicago Press, 1953), pp. 267 (note 32), 275–76.

² See Pierre Burgelin, *La Philosophie de l'existence de J-J Rousseau* (Paris: Presses Universitaires de France, 1952), pp. 205–8; Lester G. Crocker, *Jean-Jacques Rousseau: The Quest (1712–1758)* (New York: Macmillan, 1968), p. 256; Emile Durkheim, *Montesquieu et Rousseau: Précurseurs de la Sociologie* (Paris: Marcel Rivière, 1953), pp. 116–20; Jean Terrasse, *Jean-Jacques Rousseau et la quête de l'âge d'or* (Brussels: Palais des académies, 1970), pp. 68–85.

³ See Robert Derathé, *Jean-Jacques Rousseau et la science politique de son temps* (Paris: Presses Universitaires de France, 1950), pp. 126–27. Derathé indicates that he follows the interpretation of C. E. Vaughan, *Studies in the History of Political Philosophy Before and After Rousseau*, 2 vols. (New York: Russell and Russell, 1960), 1:28–30. The most striking statement that Rousseau was himself confused on this point is found in Ernst Cassirer, *Rousseau, Kant, Goethe*, trans. James Guttman, Paul O. Kristeller, and John H. Randall, Jr. (Hamden, Conn.: Archon Books, 1961), p. 24. Cassirer seems to have pulled back from his earlier view, expressed in *The Question of Jean-Jacques Rousseau*, trans. Peter Gay (New York: Columbia University Press, 1954), p. 50, that Rousseau intended the state of nature to be purely hypothetical.

⁴ See Jean Guéhenno, *Jean-Jacques Rousseau*, trans. John and Doreen Weightman, 2 vols. (London: Routledge & Kegan Paul, 1966), 1:292–94. Guéhenno gives a clear statement of these scientific concerns, though he seems to incline against the view that Rousseau's state of nature is meant to be historical.

⁵ *Second Discourse*, pp. 103–4 [P, 3:133].

⁶ Ibid., pp. 92–93 [P, 3:123] (italics mine).

⁷ The main body of the text of the *Second Discourse* is preceded by a Dedication and a Preface and is followed by a series of Notes. The *Discourse* proper is divided into a First Part and a Second Part of approximately equal length, but the First Part does not begin immediately at the conclusion of the Preface. Instead, the main body of the text begins with an introductory section of a few pages, a kind of second preface. Hereafter this unlabeled section will be referred to as the Introduction.

⁸ *Second Discourse*, pp. 102–3 [P, 3:132–33].

⁹ See Havens, "Diderot, Rousseau," for a discussion of how precarious Rousseau's situation vis-à-vis the authorities had already become during the time he was working on the *Second Discourse*. Havens also presents an excellent account of the character of censorship during this period, how it influenced the entire intellectual atmosphere, and how it affected the forms of literary production.

¹⁰ The thesis of the Abbé de Prades, containing certain speculations on the origins of human knowledge and human society, was defended before the Sorbonne in November 1751 and then censured by the Faculty of Theology on 27 January 1752, and by the Archbishop of Paris on 29 January 1752. Diderot, who was falsely accused of being the true author of the original thesis, wrote part of the *Apologie de l'Abbé de Prades* in the Abbé's name. In the *Apologie*, Diderot defends the Abbé against the accusation of having "substituted a fantastic being for the man of *Genesis*." Despite all the eloquence of Diderot, the Abbé de Prades was condemned and fled the country. See Diderot, *Oeuvres Complètes*, ed., J. Assézat, 20 vols. (Paris, 1875–77), 1:429–84.

¹¹ Morel, "Recherches sur les sources," p. 135.

¹² Havens, "Diderot, Rousseau," p. 261. See also pp. 231, 233.

13 See Otis Fellows, "Buffon and Rousseau: Aspects of a Relationship," *Publications of the Modern Language Association of America* 75, no. 3 (June 1960): 192; Guéhenno, *Jean-Jacques Rousseau*, 1:294 (note 1); Lovejoy, "Supposed Primitivism," p. 19 (note 4); Strauss, *Natural Right and History*, p. 267 (note 32). For a more general discussion of this phenomenon, see Strauss, *Persecution and the Art of Writing* (Glencoe, Ill: Free Press, 1952).

14 *Emile*, P, 4:606–35.

15 *Second Discourse*, pp. 103–4 [P, 3:133].

16 In this connection, see also Note J of the *Second Discourse*, pp. 210–11 [P, 3:212–13], where Rousseau criticizes the ability of Christian missionaries to study men and praises the ancient pagan philosophers who voyaged to "shake off the yoke of national prejudices . . . and to acquire that universal knowledge which is not that of one century or one country exclusively, but which, being of all times and all places, is so to speak the common science of the wise."

17 This interpretation is supported by the analysis of revelation presented by the Savoyard Vicar in Rousseau's *Emile* (P, 4:610): "Apôtre de la verité, qu'avez-vous donc à me dire dont je ne reste pas le juge? Dieu lui-même a parlé; écoutez sa révélation. C'est autre chose. Dieu a parlé! Voila certe un grand mot. Et à qui a-t-il parlé? Il a parlé aux hommes. Pourquoi donc n'en ai je rien entendu? Il a chargé d'autres hommes de vous rendre sa parole. J'entends: ce sont des hommes qui vont me dire ce que Dieu a dit. J'aimerois mieux avoir entendu Dieu lui-même; il ne lui en auroit pas coûté davantage, et j'aurois été à l'abri de la séduction. Il vous en garantit en manifestant la mission de ses envoyés. Comment cela? Par des prodiges. Et où sont ces prodiges? *Dans des livres. Et qui a fait ces livres? Des hommes.* Et qui a vu ces prodiges? Des hommes qui les attestent. Quoi! toujours des témoignages humains? Toujours des hommes qui me raportent ce que d'autres hommes ont rapporté!" (italics mine).

18 *Second Discourse*, p. 141 [P, 3:162] (italics mine).

19 An anonymous critic of the *Second Discourse*, writing in *L'Année Littéraire*, vol. 7, Lettre 7 (n.p., 1755), finds evidence of the insincerity of Rousseau's obeissance to the Biblical teaching

Notes# Notes

in the formulation of his very first statement that the state of nature may never have existed: " 'L'état de nature, dit-il [Rousseau], n'existe plus, n'existera probablement jamais & n'a peut-être jamais existé. . . . Il faut nier que les hommes se soient jamais trouvés dans le pur état de nature. . . .' S'il faut nier absolument que les hommes se soient jamais trouvés dans l'état de nature, pourquoi dire que cet état n'a peut-être jamais existé; ce *peut-être* est assûrement de trop" (pp. 148–49, italics in the original).

20 *Second Discourse*, p. 93 [P, 3:123–24] (italics in the original).

21 In suggesting toward the end of the Preface (p. 95 [P, 3:125] that "all scientific books which teach us only to see men as they have made themselves" be left aside, Rousseau is apparently referring to the books of the natural law theorists. He continues to support his arguments with quotes drawn from the *Histoire naturelle* of Buffon.

22 *Second Discourse*, Note L, p. 215 [P, 3:215]. See also Note D, p. 186 [P, 3:198].

23 Ibid., p. 103 [P, 3:133].

24 Morel, "Recherches sur les sources," p. 198 (italics mine).

25 *Second Discourse*, p. 98 [P, 3:128].

26 On the importance of the Notes, see also Masters, *Political Philosophy of Rousseau*, pp. 108–9.

27 *Second Discourse*, p. 141 [P, 3:163].

28 Ibid., p. 103 [P, 3:133].

29 *First Discourse*, pp. 60–64 [P, 3:27–30].

30 *Second Discourse*, Note J, p. 211 [P, 3:213].

31 For a full discussion of Rousseau's mode of writing and its relation to his philosophy, see Leo Strauss, "On the Intention of Rousseau," *Social Research* 14, no. 4 (December 1947): 455–87; see also Strauss, *Natural Right and History*, pp. 258–63, and Masters, *Political Philosophy of Rousseau*, pp. 106–11.

32 Samuel Butler, *Evolution Old and New* (London: Jonathan Cape, 1924), pp. 70–71. See chapters 9–11 of this work for But-

ler's application of this insight to the interpretation of Buffon's teaching. Butler himself does *not* suggest that this kind of writing was practiced by Buffon's famous contemporaries (including Rousseau).

[33] Arthur Lovejoy, the only commentator I have found who has recognized the importance of Note J for the understanding of Rousseau's state of nature, states: "Those who set forth the doctrine of the *Discourse* in the manner still usual in histories of literature, philosophy and political theory, must be supposed *to have neglected to read, or to have entirely forgotten Rousseau's Note J*" (Lovejoy, "Supposed Primitivism," p. 17; italics mine).

[34] *Second Discourse*, Note J, p. 204 [P, 3:208].

[35] Ibid., Note J, p. 209 [P, 3:211] (italics mine).

[36] Jean de Castillon, *Discours sur l'origine de l'inégalité parmi les hommes—pour servir de réponse au Discours que M. Rousseau, Citoyen de Genève, a publié sur le même sujet* (Amsterdam, 1756), p. xv.

3

Metaphysics

THE ARGUMENT OF the preceding chapter has shown
that Rousseau was forced to present his teaching about
the state of nature as hypothetical because it conflicted with
Christian doctrine. For the same reason, he sometimes also presents his picture of human society as hypothetical. The state
of nature teaching is hypothetical because it abstracts from
"the supernatural gifts" man received from God[1]; similarly,
the account of society shows "what we *would have become*
abandoned to ourselves" (i.e., without the beneficence of
God).[2] By means of this procedure, Rousseau is able to give
his own teaching the appearance of not being in conflict with
the Bible or with the sacred character of the existing regimes
of Christendom.

In other words, Rousseau indicates that the role of God is
crucial both for man's past and for man's present—yet his own
account of man's past and present explicitly ignores the role
of God. Can such a procedure possibly be legitimate within
the context of a serious belief in the Christian God? Precisely
this kind of objection, to which our unbelieving age is not

likely to pay much attention, was raised by Jean de Castillon. A mathematician and a philosopher, Castillon (iin his own *Discourse on the Origin of Inequality Among Men, to serve as a response to the Discourse that M. Rousseau, Citizen of Geneva, has published on the same subject*) does not rely upon the authority of the Bible. Rather, he asserts:

> I have often had recourse to the Divinity, because the nature of things has often led me there, and because I have learned from Seneca that the duty of philosophy is to search for the truth not only in human things, but also in divine things.[3]

Castillon sees, as any reader of Rousseau's *Discourse* can hardly fail to see, that Rousseau's hypothetical present is intended to represent the actual present: "We are promised man such as he might have become, and we are shown him such as he has become."[4] And he does not attempt to counter Rousseau's evaluation of contemporary society by asserting the divine right of Christian monarchs. He is willing to let the issue be decided on the question of what is natural (i.e., on Rousseau's own ground):

> If nature sanctions the inequalities that reign among us, society is just; . . . the religion that best enumerates its duties . . . is divine, if it comes from Heaven; and if its origin is less noble, it is still the most excellent instruction in morality (*cours de morale*), sustained by an authority respectable to the philosopher and necessary for the people. . . . But if these inequalities are contrary to nature, the society that requires them is a frightful brigandage, and the religion that sanctions them is a detestable imposture.[5]

Everything, then, turns on the question of what man's natural state is. And it is on this point that Castillon asserts that Rousseau's fundamental error stems from his neglect of God:

How then can we discover [man's] original condition, except by the knowledge of his creator (*auteur*)? If this philosopher [Rousseau] had followed this route, he would not have needed so many hypotheses, and he would have perceived either that one of the two facts he regards as given is not a fact, or that it is not necessary to connect these two facts. Here are the two alleged facts: Men are naturally equal; men at the present time are unequal. If the natural equality of men is made to consist in the state of dispersion and independence, this is not a fact; it is a proposition that is in need of proof, and whose truth or falsity would have been plainly revealed by considering the creator (*auteur*) of men.[6]

Here Castillon points to the central mystery of the *Second Discourse*. Referring to the crucial last paragraph of the First Part of the *Discourse*,[7] Castillon indicates that Rousseau understands both his state of nature and his state of society as "facts." There is no problem in seeing why the state of society—that is, men living in the conditions of inequality of Rousseau's own time—should be regarded as a fact. But how can Rousseau's state of nature—that is, men living in a primitive condition of equality and independence—be accorded the status of a fact? This is perhaps the most puzzling aspect of the *Second Discourse* as a whole. For time and again Rousseau emphasizes the extreme difficulty of explaining how men progressed through particular stages from their primitive state to the point at which one sees them now. The stage that is the hardest to account for is the invention of language, a problem that Rousseau dwells upon at length without resolving it to his own satisfaction. He concludes his discussion of this subject as follows:

For myself, frightened by the multiplying difficulties, and convinced of the almost demonstrated impossibility that language could have arisen and been established by purely hu-

[*33*]

man means, I leave to whomever would undertake it the discussion of the following difficult problem: Which was most necessary, previously formed society for the institution of languages; or previously invented languages for the establishment of society?[8]

And yet the question of language is a decisive one. For the essence of Rousseau's criticism of the description of man in the state of nature given by Hobbes and other modern philosophers is that they did not go back far enough, and therefore they attributed to natural man characteristics he could have acquired only in society. Hobbes correctly viewed natural man as asocial, but he mistakenly endowed him with the power of speech. Rousseau argues that speech and society go together, that speech cannot be natural to an asocial being. On the other hand, however, he seems to admit that it is all but impossible to explain how an asocial being could ever *become* a speaking being. Yet man in his present state is unquestionably a speaking being. It would appear to follow, therefore, that man must be naturally social or political.[9] In short, given Rousseau's acknowledgment of the near impossibility of explaining how asocial man could learn to speak, and given his manifest unwillingness to accept the Christian teaching that man is endowed with the gift of speech by his Creator, he would seemingly be led back to the Aristotelian view that speech is natural to man and the decisive proof of his natural sociality.

The Origins of Man

Yet Rousseau refuses to embrace the Aristotelian alternative and sticks to his contention that natural man is neither a speaking being nor a social being. To understand why he does so, it is necessary to raise a question about which Rousseau himself maintains a studied silence: the question of man's origins. Rousseau does not accept the Aristotelian view because he cannot accept its metaphysical premise—the eternity of the species (including the human species). Rousseau agrees with Christian doctrine in so far as he holds that the world and the human race are not eternal—that is, that they have come into being. But in the *Second Discourse*, Rousseau does not admit the *divine* creation of man. For this reason, at the very outset of his critique Castillon (who points out the numerous aspects in which the account of man's development in the *Second Discourse* resembles the account given by Lucretius in *De Rerum Natura*) imputes to Rousseau the Epicurean view of man's origins: ". . . he revives the deliriums of the Epicureans about our origins."[10] And later he adds, "Such is the body of the man of Rousseau, I would say of Lucretius, if the philosopher did not pass over in silence the origin of the human race, whose birth the poet attributes to the heat and humidity of the primitive earth."[11]

Castillon is on the right track in attributing to Rousseau a materialistic view of man's origins. But the internal evidence of the *Second Discourse* indicates that Rousseau follows not Epicurean physics but the mechanistic physics of the moderns. Rousseau compares the reasoning behind his inquiry into the formation of human society to the reasoning of contemporary physicists in their inquiries into the formation of the world.[12] He adopts the Cartesian doctrine that animals are machines (rather than the Epicurean view that animals possess free will and a material soul), and he suggests that all those phenomena that are not "purely spiritual" can be explained by the laws of mechanics.[13] The key to his explanation of how natural man was able to progress to the point at which he has now arrived is "the surprising power of very trivial causes when they act without interruption" over long periods of time.[14] All the differences among men (as among the other species of animals) can be traced back to "successive changes in the human constitution" prompted by "various physical causes":

In effect, it is not conceivable that these first changes, by whatever means they occurred, altered all at once and in the same way all the individuals of the species; but some, being perfected or deteriorated and having acquired diverse qualities, good or bad, which were not inherent in their nature, the others remained longer in their original state. And such was the first source of inequality among men, which is more easily demonstrated thus in general than assigned its true causes with precision.[15]

If, then, Rousseau adopts the mechanistic explanation of the "physicists" to account for man's "progress," it would seem highly likely that he also accepts a mechanistic account of man's origins. Confirmation for this suggestion can be found in the one place in the *Second Discourse* where Rousseau does explicitly (though fleetingly) broach the question of man's origins—the very first paragraph of the First Part:

Important as it may be, in order to judge the natural state of man correctly, to consider him from his origin and examine him, so to speak, in the first embryo of the species, I shall not follow his organic structure through its successive developments. I shall not stop to investigate in the animal system what he could have been at the beginning in order to become at length what he is. I shall not examine whether, as Aristotle thinks, man's elongated nails were not at first hooked claws; whether he was not hairy like a bear; and whether, if he walked on all fours (C), his gaze, directed toward the earth and confined to a horizon of several paces, did not indicate both the character and the limits of his ideas. On this subject I could form only vague and almost imaginary conjectures. Comparative anatomy has as yet made too little progress and the observations of naturalists are as yet too uncertain for one to be able to establish the basis of solid reasoning upon such foundations. Thus, without having recourse to the supernatural knowledge we have on this point, and without regard to the changes that must have come about in the internal as well as external conformation of man as he applied his limbs to new uses and as he nourished himself on new foods, I shall suppose him to have been formed from all time as I see him today: walking on two feet, using his hands as we do ours, directing his gaze on all of nature, and measuring the vast expanse of heaven with his eyes.[16]

Here Rousseau suggests an evolutionary explanation of man's beginnings. Man emerged from a lower point in the "animal system" by "successive developments" in his "organic structure." In the years immediately preceding the composition of the *Second Discourse*, this "transformist" doctrine had been advanced (with similar caution) by both Diderot and Buffon, two men whose influence on Rousseau is unquestioned. It is known from Rousseau's own testimony in his *Confessions* that Diderot advised him during the writing of the *Second Discourse*, and Buffon is the author most frequently cited in the *Discourse*.[17]

It is true, of course, that Rousseau explicitly withholds judgment on the validity of the evolutionary theory, but the reason that he offers for this suspension of judgment is merely the undeveloped state of the science of comparative anatomy. In a note to this passage (Note C), Rousseau rejects the view that man is naturally a quadruped, but he bases his arguments there on the incompatibility between human anatomy and the anatomy of quadrupeds.[18] This argument merely shows that man's conformation is that of a biped; it does not show that man could not have acquired his present conformation as a result of a gradual development from creatures that had a different structure. And in fact, toward the end of the passage quoted above, *after* he has indicated the "uncertain" character of the transformist doctrine, he speaks of "the changes that *must* have come about in the internal as well as external conformation of man as he applied his limbs to new uses and as he nourished himself on new foods" (italics mine).

[*37*]

In other words, it would appear that Rousseau's hesitancy to openly embrace a transformist theory must be attributed primarily to his wariness of the ecclesiastical authorities. For only the acceptance of the premise that man gradually emerged by natural (i.e., physical) causes from that which is subhuman gives plausibility to Rousseau's account of the state of nature. Only on the basis of such a view of man's origins can it be regarded as a fact that natural man does not possess speech or reason.

Lest this line of reasoning sound strange to us, it should be remembered that it constitutes the all but unquestioned dogma of our own day. Modern science still has not succeeded in unraveling the mystery of the invention and development of speech. But because we accept the premise that man gradually emerged from lower (i.e., nonspeaking) animals, and because we refuse to admit any supernatural or otherwise nonnatural causes, we do not for a moment doubt that speech was acquired by man himself at some point during *human* history. For it would be unreasonable—given the principles of our science—to assert that when creatures whose bodily conformation one would recognize as essentially "human" first emerged upon the earth, they suddenly possessed the ability to speak. So we, like Rousseau, take it as a given fact that the first men did not possess language.

Beast or God?

The plausibility of Rousseau's account of the state of nature rests, then, on the view that man gradually emerged from that which is lower than man in the natural order. The clear implication of this view is that man in his natural (i.e., original) condition is fundamentally a beast like any other. This interpretation—that Rousseau's natural man is a brute—was made by a number of contemporary critics of the *Second Discourse*. In a famous letter to Rousseau, Voltaire remarked of the *Sec-*

ond Discourse, "Never before has anyone employed so much genius in wishing to turn us into beasts."[19] Castillon asserts that Rousseau "reduced our first fathers to the level of the most stupid beasts,"[20] and that Rousseau's state of nature "makes men as similar as possible to the brutes."[21] Finally, an anonymous critic, writing in *L'Année Littéraire* of 1755, states: "The bold La Mettrie wrote a book (*l'Homme machine*) in which he made an effort to prove that man is only a machine. M. Rousseau today presents us with the beast-man (*l'homme bête*)."[22]

In the *Second Discourse*, Rousseau carefully avoids directly asserting that original men are indistinguishable from brutes. And indeed, the question of the differences and similarities between men and beasts occurs prominently in several places throughout the work: Toward the end of the Preface, Rousseau addresses the question of whether animals participate in natural law.[23] In the First Part of the *Discourse*, he investigates the "specific distinction" of man among the other animals.[24] And he devotes the important Note J to a discussion of the possibility that unskillful observers may have regarded as beasts of another species creatures that are really primitive men.[25] In fact, this critical issue is broached, albeit in more subtle form, in the very first paragraph of the Preface, where Rousseau makes the following comparison:

> Like the statue of Glaucus, which time, sea, and storms had so disfigured that it looked less like a god than a wild beast, the human soul, altered in the bosom of society by a thousand continually renewed causes, by the acquisition of a mass of knowledge and errors, by changes that occurred in the constitution of bodies, and by the continual impact of the passions, has, so to speak, changed its appearance to the point of being nearly unrecognizable. . . .[26]

The Greek sea god Glaucus had first been used as an image of the human soul by Plato in Book 10 of the *Republic*. There, in attempting to prove to Glaucon that the soul is immortal, Socrates asserts that because we have experience of the soul only as it is linked with the body, we do not appreciate the true divinity of its nature:

> Just as those who catch sight of the sea Glaucus would no longer easily see his original nature because some of the old parts of his body have been broken off and the others have been ground down and thoroughly maimed by the waves at the same time as other things have grown on him—shells, seaweed, and rocks—so that he resembles any beast rather than what he was by nature, so, too, we see the soul in such a condition because of countless evils.[27]

Though Rousseau speaks of the soul as being disfigured by various historical developments rather than by its junction with the body, he otherwise seems, at first glance, to be using this analogy essentially in the spirit of Plato: The soul in its pristine character is godlike, but when it is contaminated by external factors, it can appear more like a wild beast than like a god. This would suggest that, for Rousseau, man in his pristine state (i.e., in the state of nature) would resemble a god—but no reader of the *Second Discourse* could conclude that Rousseau's natural man, whose "first care [is] that of his preservation,"[28] is godlike. In fact, Rousseau's description of man in his natural state would seem to support the contention that the human "soul" in its pristine state resembles precisely a wild beast. Rousseau even refers explicitly to primitive men's ability to defend themselves against "*other* wild beasts":[29]

> Pit a bear or a wolf against a savage who is robust, agile, courageous, as they all are, armed with stones and a good stick, and you will see that the danger will be reciprocal at the very least, and that after several similar experiences *wild beasts, which do not like to attack each other, will hardly attack man willingly, having found him to be just as wild as they.*[30]

Metaphysics

Matter and Spirit

The First Part of the *Second Discourse* describes man in his original state. Rousseau indicates that this part can be further divided into two subsections, the first of which deals with "physical man" (*l'homme physique*) and the second of which examines natural man "from the metaphysical and moral side."[31] He states this principle of organization only at the conclusion of the first subsection, which attempts to prove that if men led a purely animal-like existence—that is, if they enjoyed none of the benefits that come from society and reason —they would be able to survive in this condition as well as animals of other species. But by explicitly stating his intention to look at original man from the moral and metaphysical side as well, Rousseau seems to suggest that a purely physical account of natural man is insufficient, and the reader of the *Second Discourse* is naturally led to expect that a much more traditional and human depiction of natural man will follow. It is highly questionable, however, whether what actually follows fulfills such an expectation. Therefore, it is necessary to investigate whether Rousseau actually does introduce any fundamentally new principles in his "metaphysical and moral" discussion of natural man (i.e., whether he really does proceed in accordance with the premise that the first men are essentially different from other animals), or whether the following statement by the anonymous critic of *L'Année Littéraire* does not get closer to the truth:

> In his savage man, M. Rousseau finds two of them, the physical savage man, and the metaphysical and moral savage man. This is as if one spoke of the physical bear, and the metaphysical and moral bear. . . .[32]

Rousseau begins his metaphysical discussion of man by affirming the Cartesian doctrine that all animals are merely "ingenious machines." What makes the "human machine" distinctive is that while "nature alone does everything in the operations of a beast . . . man contributes to his operations as a free agent." Rousseau goes out of his way to make it clear that it is his freedom, *and not his understanding*, that constitutes the "specific distinction" of man and shows the spirituality of his soul. For "the formation of ideas," of which beasts as well as men are capable, can be explained by mechanistic physics. The difference between man and beast in this regard, therefore, is one of degree rather than of substance.[33]

In explicitly accepting a mechanistic explanation of human thought, Rousseau takes one decisive step beyond the explicit teaching of Descartes. In the Fifth Part of the *Discourse on Method*, where Descartes first presents his doctrine that animals are machines and that the human *body* is also a machine, he indicates "two very certain ways" in which it can be proved that men are not merely machines.[34] The first of these involves man's ability to speak and the second his ability to use reason.[35] In other words, the difference between man and the animals lies in man's understanding, which cannot be explained mechanistically (i.e., as an attribute of matter). And it is a central point of Descartes's doctrine, of course, that thinking is the specific activity of the soul, that purely spiritual substance which is found only in man. So the description of the soul presented in the *Second Discourse* cannot be based on Cartesian metaphysics.

By the same token, the argument of the *Second Discourse* is incompatible with the metaphysics set forth in the "Profession of Faith of a Savoyard Vicar" in Rousseau's own *Emile*.[36] For the Savoyard Vicar accepts the Cartesian contention that thought cannot be an attribute of matter, that only an immaterial substance is capable of thinking.[37] Moreover, the Savoyard Vicar seems inclined to view the motion of animals as spontaneous, that is, inexplicable by the laws of mechanics.[38]

In other words, he rejects the Cartesian doctrine that animals are machines, which is central to the metaphysics of the *Second Discourse*. The Savoyard Vicar attributes less power to matter than did Descartes; the *Second Discourse* attributes more power to matter than did Descartes. It is not surprising, therefore, that the moral teaching of the Savoyard Vicar will also differ from the moral teaching of the *Second Discourse*.[39]

What, then, is one to make of these inconsistencies between the *Second Discourse* and the "Profession of Faith of a Savoyard Vicar"? A complete explanation of them (or of other apparent discrepancies between the *Second Discourse* and the *Emile*) would presuppose a full interpretation of the *Emile*, Rousseau's most complex and difficult work, and hence is beyond the scope of this essay. But, broadly speaking, such inconsistencies can be explained in one of two ways. The first would hold that Rousseau changed his views after writing the *Second Discourse*; the second would hold that Rousseau expressed himself differently in accordance with the differing intentions animating these two works. In the light of Rousseau's various statements affirming the unity underlying all his writings,[40] it seems more prudent to follow the latter approach in seeking a provisional explanation of the inconsistencies detailed above.

First of all, Rousseau distances himself from the ideas expressed in the "Profession of Faith" by putting them in the mouth of a fictional character.[41] And at the conclusion of the vicar's statement of the principles of his "natural religion," Rousseau, speaking in his own voice, indicates that he sees "hosts of objections" that could be made.[42] The "Profession of Faith" is presented in the context of the moral education of the adolescent Emile. It culminates in the proposition that the soul—which is immaterial—survives the body, and therefore "Providence is justified."[43] Rousseau thus indicates that the belief in an afterlife is a necessary prop to the morality of "men with ordinary minds" (*les esprits vulgaires*)—a class to which Emile belongs[44]—who live in society.

It should be remembered that the Platonic argument that Rousseau alludes to by referring to the Greek god Glaucus is also a proof of the immortality of the soul.[45] Similarly, Descartes's proof of the specific distinction between men and beasts in Part Five of the *Discourse on Method* has the explicit intention of showing that the human soul is immortal and of thereby keeping "men with weak minds" (*les esprits faibles*) on the path of virtue.[46] But in the *Second Discourse* Rousseau makes no attempt to argue for the immortality of the soul. The *Second Discourse* is meant to be a "scientific" work; it is that work in which, by his own avowal, Rousseau's principles "are revealed with the greatest boldness not to say audacity."[47] It is the *Second Discourse*, then, which should be taken as the most revealing statement of Rousseau's metaphysics.

At the same time, however, the *Second Discourse*, which Rousseau dedicated to his fellow citizens of Geneva, also is a work with a political intention. As such, it must avoid destroying those beliefs that are necessary for preserving a decent political life. In the *Social Contract*, where he affirms the necessity of a "civil profession of faith," Rousseau indicates that among these necessary dogmas is a belief in the life to come.[48] So even apart from his fear of persecution, Rousseau's understanding of the needs of political life would prevent him from openly denying the immateriality of the soul.[49]

It is for these reasons that Rousseau in the *Second Discourse* gives the appearance of upholding a kind of dualist metaphysics by suggesting that human liberty proves the spirituality of the human soul. For in itself, the argument that human thought can be explained mechanistically, while human choice is purely spiritual, is clearly untenable. This difficulty was pointed out by Castillon, who argues that if man has a soul that is spiritual in nature, it must be the source of his understanding as well as of his liberty.

> Liberty, [Rousseau] says, shows the spirituality of the soul. Our choice is often ruled by reasons (*motifs*) that certainly are perceived by the principle which wills, since they influence its determinations. Thus the spiritual soul is also capable of thinking. Therefore it is pointless to suppose a thinking being different from the spiritual soul. . . .[50]

And Rousseau's Savoyard Vicar similarly points to the intimate and interdependent relation between human liberty and human understanding:

> When I am asked what cause determines my will, I ask in turn what cause determines my judgment; for it is clear that these two causes add up to only one, and if it is understood that man is active in his judgments, that his understanding is only the power of comparing and judging, it will be seen that his liberty is only a similar or derivative power. He chooses the good as he has judged the true; if he judges falsely, he chooses badly. What then is the cause that determines his will? It is his judgment. And what is the cause that determines his judgment? It is his faculty of intelligence. . . .[51]

Even in the *Second Discourse* itself, Rousseau acknowledges the problems that beset this peculiar sort of dualism:

> But if the difficulties surrounding all these questions should leave some room for dispute on this difference between man and animal, there is another very specific quality that distinguishes them and about which there can be no dispute: the faculty of self-perfection, a faculty which, with the aid of circumstances, successively develops all the others, and resides among us as much in the species as in the individual.[52]

The remainder of the *Second Discourse* is in no way dependent upon the metaphysical premises of human free will and the spirituality of the human soul.[53] Instead, it starts from the premise of human perfectibility, which Rousseau never states to be inexplicable by the laws of mechanics.

Perfectibility

In introducing the notion of human perfectibility, Rousseau describes it as a "faculty," one which "with the aid of circumstances, successively develops all the others." In this context, as the rest of the *Second Discourse* makes clear, "the others" include reason, language, the social virtues, and similar attributes of civilized man that are not operative in the state of nature. Because these faculties are not operative in original men, they are not cited as constituting the specific distinction of man, and this title is instead assigned to perfectibility.

But this raises a question as to just what the status of these other faculties is: Can they in any sense be considered natural? Rousseau leaves the answer to this question shrouded in ambiguity. At first, he appears to refer to them as "natural."[54] Yet in the two passages where he addresses this question most directly, he qualifies this characterization by referring to these faculties as ones that belong to men "in potentiality" (*en puissance*). In the first of these two passages, he attributes the fact that these faculties "develop only with the opportunities to exercise them" to "a very wise providence."[55] This might still seem to be compatible with the view that they are somehow part of man's natural endowment: All men possess the faculty, say, of reason, but under some conditions this faculty may not become operative.

In the second of these passages, however, Rousseau emphasizes that these faculties "could never develop by themselves, that in order to develop they needed the *chance* combination of several foreign causes *which might never have arisen* and without which . . . [natural man] would have remained eter-

nally in his primitive condition. . . ."[56] But if the development
of these faculties is due not to providence but to chance, and
if without certain accidental occurrences they would have remained eternally inoperative, it is hard to understand how they
could be said to be part of man's natural endowment at all,
even if only "in potentiality."[57] This impression is reinforced
by a statement that Rousseau makes earlier in the First Part:
". . . [F]rom the little care taken by nature to bring men together through mutual needs and to facilitate their use of
speech one at least sees how little it prepared their sociability,
and how little it contributed to everything men have done to
establish social bonds."[58] One is forced to conclude, then, that
all these human attributes that involve human sociability are
more aptly described by Rousseau in still another passage of
the *Second Discourse*, where he calls them "artificial faculties,"
and implies that man did not receive them at all from "the
hands of nature."[59] Yet if this is true, Rousseau's very use of
the term "faculties" in this context becomes questionable, as
Castillon's criticism of him on this point indicates: "Art can
very well facilitate the exercise of the faculties; but it does not
produce (*donne*) them; it can very well extend them; but not
create them. An artificial faculty is a contradiction, unless one
confuses the faculty with its perfection."[60] The very notion
of a faculty, in its traditional philosophical usage, means something that is intended by nature to perform a certain function.[61]
And as Rousseau indicates that nature has done so little to make
possible the development of reason, language, and the social
virtues, these attributes of civilized man cannot properly be
considered faculties at all.

But what about perfectibility itself? Can it properly be
considered a faculty in the precise sense? In order to answer
this question, it is first necessary to examine the question of
whether human perfectibility is always operative in man's natural state. Because perfectibility is Rousseau's explanation of

how man was able to progress beyond the state of nature, it
would seem that perfectibility must be operative in original
man. Yet a close look at the text reveals that this is not the case.
In his first statement of how perfectibility distinguishes the human species from an animal species, he emphasizes that the latter would be "at the end of a thousand years what it was the
first year of that thousand."[62] Yet later Rousseau characterizes
man in the state of nature as follows:

> There was neither education nor progress; the generations
> multiplied uselessly; and everyone always starting from the
> same point, centuries passed in all the crudeness of the first
> ages; the species was already old, and man remained ever a
> child.[63]

Similarly, in Note J, by suggesting the possibility that "various
animals similar to men" might really be men who "had *not acquired any degree of perfection*, and [were] still found in the
primitive state of nature,"[64] Rousseau indicates that perfectibility may very well remain inoperative among men in their
original condition. This is confirmed toward the end of the
First Part, where Rousseau includes perfectibility among those
faculties that man has received "in potentiality" and that depend on chance for their development.[65]

One is forced to conclude, then, that perfectibility also
cannot be understood in terms of the traditional notion of a
"faculty," for it does not perform a function that is intended
by nature. If perfectibility were a faculty in the proper sense,
then human society, as the natural outcome of this faculty,
would itself be natural. Precisely this argument was urged
against Rousseau by another contemporary critic of the *Second Discourse*, Rousseau's fellow Genevan Charles Bonnet,
writing under the pseudonym of Philopolis. Philopolis argues
as follows:

Everything which results immediately from the *faculties* of man, must it not be said to result from his *nature*? Yet I believe it has been very clearly demonstrated that the *state of society* results immediately from the faculties of man; I do not wish to cite any proofs for our author other than his own ideas on the establishment of societies—ingenious ideas that he has so elegantly expressed in the Second Part of his *Discourse*. If, then, the *state of society* derives (*découle*) from the faculties of man, it is *natural* to man. It would thus be as unreasonable to complain because these faculties, in developing, have given birth to this state, as it would be to complain because God has given man such faculties.

Man is [a being] such as the place he should occupy in the universe requires. It apparently was necessary that there be men who build cities, just as it was necessary that there be beavers who build lodges. This *perfectibility* which Rousseau holds to be the characteristic that essentially distinguishes man from the brutes must, by the author's own avowal, conduct man to the point where we see him today. To wish that this were not so would be to wish that man were not *man*; does the eagle which disappears in the clouds crawl in the dust like the serpent? [66]

Here is the essential part of Rousseau's reply:

Since you claim to attack me by my own system, do not forget, I pray you, that according to me society is natural to the human species as decrepitude is to the individual, and that arts, laws, and governments are necessary for peoples, as crutches are necessary for the old. The only difference is that the state of old age derives (*découle*) solely from the nature of man and that the state of society derives (*découle*) from the nature of the human race, not immediately, as you say, but only, as I have proved, with the aid of certain external (*extérieures*) circumstances that could have occurred or not occurred (*qui pouvoient être ou n'être pas*), or at least happened sooner or later and consequently accelerated or slowed down its progress.[67]

As a careful reading of this exchange shows, Rousseau's concept of perfectibility, with its dependence on the chance workings of external causes, makes sense only in terms of the mechanistic understanding of nature supplied by modern science. It is simply incompatible with the traditional doctrine of the faculties (here espoused by Philopolis), which is bound up with a teleological understanding of nature.[68] By speaking of perfectibility, reason, and the like as "faculties," Rousseau follows his great predecessor John Locke in presenting his new understanding of man "clothed in the ordinary fashion and language of the country."[69] Man can indeed be characterized by perfectibility since he alone among the species has progressed beyond his animal beginnings. But for that progress man is not beholden to nature. Man's specific distinction can no longer be understood as a natural distinction. It is one that has emerged over time, due to the chance workings of mechanical causation. (If something about man's physical makeup, such as his upright posture, is a necessary condition of his progress, it too must be understood as a product of mechanical causation, in no way implying that the attributes of civilized man were *intended* by nature. Indeed, from a metaphysical point of view, to find the specific distinction of man in his perfectibility amounts to much the same thing as finding it in his upright posture, his opposable thumb, or his larger brain. These may be necessary conditions of man's development of reason, but our science does not see in them any evidence that reason belongs to man's nature.)

The key to man's perfectibility, as Rousseau makes clear from the outset, is indeed the development of reason. (The savage who binds pieces of wood on the temples of his children, he implies, stifles their perfectibility by stifling their reason.)[70] In a sense then, for Rousseau too, reason characterizes man as we know him. Yet man's understanding originally differs from that of beasts only in degree. Reason can emerge only with the use of speech, and "speech itself is . . . not natural to [man]."[71] Reason, then, cannot be natural to man, and its origins are to be found in "the different accidents" that brought man out of his natural condition. In the Fifth Part of the *Discourse on Method*, Descartes outlines a mechanistic account of the genesis of the physical universe, but treats reason as the activity of man's rational soul, which is something wholly separate from matter and whose origins cannot be explained along mechanistic lines. In the *Second Discourse*, Rousseau extends Descartes's mechanistic explanation to make it account for the genesis of reason itself.

The genesis of man's reason proves to be identical with the genesis of man's humanity. In the state of nature man is merely another beast. It is only through the accidental developments which perfect his reason that man *becomes* human.[72] But if man's humanity is the product of a finite succession of events, rather than of his essential and unchanging nature, the record of those events becomes a decisive source for understanding his humanity. In short, man's humanity is the product of his history. To say man is the being characterized by perfectibility is to say that man as we know him is the *historical* being. Rousseau in the *Second Discourse* is the first philosopher to indicate that the modern scientific view of man's origin and man's nature must lead to this conclusion.

Notes

1 *Second Discourse*, pp. 103, 105 [P, 3:133, 134].

2 Ibid., p. 97 [P, 3:127] (italics mine).

3 Jean de Castillon, *Discours sur l'origine de l'inégalité parmi les hommes pour servir de réponse au Discours que M. Rousseau, Citoyen de Genève, a publié sur le même sujet* (Amsterdam, 1756), pp. xxx–xxxi.

4 Ibid, p. 16.

5 Ibid., pp. 2–3.

6 Ibid., pp. 97–98.

7 *Second Discourse*, p. 141 [P, 3:162–63].

8 Ibid., p. 126 [P, 3:151].

9 Cf. Castillon, *Discours sur l'origine*, pp. 84–85: "Ma conclusion diffère de celle que Rousseau tire de ses réflexions. Puis que la nature, dit-il, a pris si peu de soins pour rapprocher les hommes par des besoins mutuels et pour leur faciliter l'usage de la parole, elle a mis bien peu du sien dans l'établissement des sociétés; elle a bien peu préparé leur sociabilité.

C'est partir d'une supposition. Patrons d'un fait. L'homme raisonne, parle, et vit en société. L'homme isolé par la nature n'auroit jamais pu ni raisonner, ni parler, ni former la société. Donc les hommes n'ont jamais été sans raisonnement, sans langage, sans société."

10 Castillon, *Discours sur l'origine*, p. vi.

11 Ibid., p. 20.

12 *Second Discourse*, p. 103 [P, 3:133].

13 Ibid., pp. 113–14 [P, 3:141–42].

14 Ibid., p. 141 [P, 3:162].

[15] Ibid., p. 92 [P, 3:123].

[16] Ibid., pp. 104–5 [P, 3:134].

[17] On Diderot's influence, see *Confessions*, P, 1:389; Jean Morel, "Recherches sur les sources du discours de l'inégalité," *Annales de la Société Jean-Jacques Rousseau* (Geneva: A. Jullien, 1909), 5: 120–43; and George R. Havens, "Diderot, Rousseau, and the *Discours sur L'Inégalité*," in Otis Fellows and Gita May, eds., *Diderot Studies* (Geneva: Librairie Droz, 1961), 3:219–62. On Buffons's influence, see *Second Discourse*, Notes B, D, G, J; Morel, "Recherches sur les sources," pp. 179–98; and Otis Fellows, "Buffon and Rousseau: Aspects of a Relationship," *Publications of the Modern Language Association of America* 75, no. 3 (June 1960): 184–96. Diderot's statement of the transformist doctrine appears in Number 58 of his *Pensées sur l'interprétation de la nature*, which was published in 1754:

"De même que dans les règnes animal et végétal, un individu commence, pour ainsi dire, s'accroît, dure, dépérit et passe; n'en serait-il pas de même des espèces entières? Si la foi ne nous apprenait que les animaux sont sortis des mains du Créateur tels que nous les voyons; et s'il était permis d'avoir la moindre incertitude sur leur commencement et sur leur fin, le philosophe abandonné à ses conjectures ne pourrait-il pas soupçonner que l'animalité avait de toute éternité ses éléments particuliers, épars et confondus dans la masse de la matière; qu'il est arrivé à ces éléments de se réunir, parce qu'il était possible que cela se fît; que l'embryon formé de ces éléments a passé par une infinité d'organisations et de développements; qu'il a eu, par succession, du mouvement, de la sensation, des idées, de la pensée, de la réflexion, de la conscience, des sentiments, des passions, des signes, des gestes, des sons, des sons articulés, une langue, des lois, des sciences, et des arts; qu'il s'est écoulé des millions d'années entre chacun de ces développements; qu'il a peut-être encore d'autres développements à subir et d'autres accroissements à prendre, qui nous sont inconnus; qu'il a eu ou qu'il aura un état stationnaire; qu'il s'éloigne ou qu'il s'éloignera de cet état par un dépérissement éternel, pendant lequel ses facultés sortiront de lui comme elles y étaient entrées; qu'il disparaîtra pour jamais de la nature, ou plutôt qu'il continuera d'y exister, mais sous une forme, et avec des facultés tout autres que celles qu'on lui remarque dans cet instant de la durée? La religion nous épargne bien des écarts et bien des travaux. Si elle ne nous eût point éclairés sur l'origine du monde et sur le système universel des êtres, combien d'hypothèses différentes que nous aurions été tentés de prendre pour le secret de la nature? Ces hypothèses étant toutes également fausses, nous auraient paru toutes à peu près également vraisemblables."

Buffon first suggested a transformist solution to the problem of species in the chapter "L'Ane," in volume 4 of his *Histoire naturelle*. This volume appeared in 1753 and is cited by Rousseau in Note G of the *Second Discourse*. The key passage reads as follows:

"Dans ce point de vue, non seulement l'âne et le cheval, mais même l'homme, le singe, les quadrupèdes et tous les animaux, pourraient être regardés comme ne faisant que la même *famille*; mais en doit-on conclure que dans cette grande et nombreuse famille, que Dieu seul a conçue et tirée du néant, il y ait d'autres petites familles projetées par la nature et produites par le temps, dont les unes ne seraient composées que de deux individus, comme le cheval et l'âne; d'autres de plusieurs individus, comme celle de la belette, de la martre, du furet, de la fouine, etc., et, de même que les végétaux, il y ait des familles de dix, vingt, trente, etc., plantes? Si ces familles existaient, en effet, elles n'auraient pu se former que par le mélange, la variation successive et la dégénération des espèces originaires; et si l'on admet une fois qu'il y ait des familles dans les plantes et dans les animaux, que l'âne soit de la famille du cheval, et qu'il n'en diffère que parce qu'il a dégénéré, on pourra dire également que le singe est de la famille de l'homme, que c'est un homme dégénéré, que l'homme et le singe ont eu une origine commune comme le cheval et l'âne, que chaque famille, tant dans les animaux que dans les végétaux, n'a eu qu'une seule souche, et même que tous les animaux sont venus d'un seul animal, que, dans la succession des temps, a produit, en se perfectionnant et en dégénérant, toutes les races des autres animaux.

"Les naturalistes, qui établissent si légèrement des familles dans les animaux et dans les végétaux, ne paraissent pas avoir assez senti toute l'étendue de ces consequences qui réduiraient le produit immédiat de la création à un nombre d'individus aussi petit que l'on voudrait: car s'il était une fois prouvé qu'on pût établir ces familles avec raison, s'il était acquis que dans les animaux, et meme dans les végétaux, il y eût, je ne dis pas plusieurs espèces, mais une seule qui eût été produite par la dégéneration d'une autre espèce; s'il était vrai que l'âne ne fût qu'un cheval dégénéré, il n'y aurait plus de bornes à la puissance de la nature, et l'on n'aurait pas tort de supposer que d'un seul être elle a su tirer avec le temps tous les autres êtres organisés.

"Mais non: il est certain, par la révélation, que tous les animaux ont également participé à la grace de la création, que les deux premiers de chaque espèce et de toutes les espèces sont sortis tout formés des mains du Créateur, et l'on doit croire qu'ils étaient tels alors, à peu près, qu'ils nous sont aujourd'hui représentés par leurs descendants."

Morel ("Recherches sur les sources," pp. 138–39) unequivocally suggests that Rousseau follows Diderot in adopting the transformist explanation: "Si l'on réfléchit que les *Pensées sur l'interprétation de la nature* paraissent en pleine composition du Discours; que Rousseau dût être associé aux hardiesses de Diderot, et a ses craintes de la censure, qu'il corrigea peut-être les épreuves avec son ami, ou se fit lire les bonnes pages, il n'est pas exagéré de dire que le *Discours est le développement de la Pensée LVIII de Diderot*" (italics in original).

Fellows ("Buffon and Rousseau," pp. 191–92) is more cautious, but argues that Rousseau would have understood as ironic the disclaimers in favor of revelation by both Diderot *and* Buffon. He also quotes the following remark by Alfred Giard, *Controverses Transformistes* (Paris: C. Naud, 1904), p. 191: "Le brillant esprit qui entrevit le premier le remarquable mécanisme de la sélection naturelle est, je crois, Jean-Jacques Rousseau."

[18] *Second Discourse*, Note C, pp. 183–86 [P, 3:196–98].

[19] Voltaire, *Lettre à Rousseau* (30 August 1755), reproduced in the Pléiade Edition of Rousseau, 3:226 (note 1).

[20] Castillon, *Discours sur l'origine*, p. vi.

[21] Ibid., p. 95.

[22] *L'Année Littéraire*, vol. 7, Lettre 7 (n.p., 1755), p. 167.

[23] *Second Discourse*, p. 96 [P, 3:126].

[24] Ibid., pp. 113–15 [P, 3:141–42].

[25] Ibid., Note J, pp. 203–13 [P, 3:208–14].

[26] Ibid., p. 91 [P, 3:122].

27 *The Republic of Plato*, trans. Allan Bloom (New York: Basic Books, 1968), p. 295 (611d).

28 *Second Discourse*, p. 142 [P, 3:164].

29 Ibid., p. 106 [P, 3:135] (italics mine).

30 Ibid., pp. 107–8 [P, 3:136] (italics mine).

31 Ibid., p. 113 [P, 3:141].

32 *L'Année Littéraire*, vol. 7 (1755), p. 152. This passage continues as follows: "... car la nourriture, le désir de la femelle et le repos font l'homme sauvage physique et l'ours physique aussi; l'instinct fait l'homme sauvage metaphysique et moral, de même que c'est l'instinct qui fait l'ours moral et metaphysique. N'allez pas rire, Monsieur, de cette comparaison; elle est juste; car M. Rousseau dit: 'Tout animal a des idées puisqu'il a des sens; il combine même ses idées jusqu'à un certain point, et l'homme ne diffère a cet égard de la bête que du plus ou moins.' Ainsi l'ours est moins homme que l'homme; l'âme de l'homme est plus âme que l'âme de l'ours! L'âme de l'ours n'est sans doute que la moitié, le tiers, le quart, ou une autre quantité quelconque moindre que la totalité de l'âme de l'homme!"

33 *Second Discourse*, pp. 113–14 [P, 3:141–42].

34 Descartes, *Discourse on Method*, Fifth Part, toward the end.

35 Cf. *Second Discourse*, Note J, p. 207 [P, 3:210], where Rousseau explicitly rejects these two ways of distinguishing man from the other animals: "... [O]ne does not see the reason the authors have for refusing to give the animals in question the name of savage men; but it is easy to guess that it is due to their stupidity and also because they did not talk: weak reasons for those who know that although the organ of speech is natural to man, speech itself is nonetheless not natural to him, and who know to what point his perfectibility can have raised civil man above his original state."

36 Masters's discussion of Rousseau's metaphysics and its relation to the rest of Rousseau's thought has the grave defect of ignoring these crucial differences between the *Emile* and the *Second Discourse*. Roger Masters, *The Political Philosophy of Rousseau* (Princeton: Princeton University Press, 1968), pp. 58–73.

37 ". . . pour moi je n'ai besoin, quoi qu'en dise Locke, de con-
noitre la matiére que comme étendue et divisible pour être assuré
qu'elle ne peut penser. . . ." *Emile*, P, 4:584.

"Une machine ne pense point, il n'y a ni mouvement ni figure
qui produise la réflexion." Ibid., P, 4:585.

38 "Vous me demanderez si les mouvemens des animaux sont
spontanés; je vous dirai que je n'en sais rien, mais que l'analogie est
pour l'affirmative." Ibid., P, 4:574.

"Ce même univers est en mouvement, et dans ses mouvemens
réglés, uniformes, assujetis à des loix constantes, il n'a rien de cette
liberté qui paroit dans les mouvemens spontanés de l'homme et des
animaux." Ibid., P, 4:575.

39 The moral teaching of the vicar is based upon the view that
man has "an innate principle of justice and virtue"—the conscience.
Rousseau's discussion of natural man in the *Second Discourse* fails
to acknowledge the existence of such an innate principle and does
not even mention the conscience. As a result, the vicar—as opposed
to Rousseau in the *Second Discourse*—is inclined to view man as by
nature sociable. See *Emile*, pp. 594–606, especially pp. 598–600; for
further discussion of these questions, see chapter 4 below.

40 See *Rousseau juge de Jean-Jacques*, P, 1:930; *Confessions*,
P, 1:406–7; *Lettre à Beaumont*, P, 4:928, 935, 950–51. This last cited
passage from the *Lettre à Beaumont* is of particular importance in
this context, as it implies the priority of the *Second Discourse* to
the *Emile*: "Quand un Auteur ne veut pas se répéter sans cesse, et
qu'il a une fois établi clairement son sentiment sur une matiere, il
n'est pas tenu de rapporter toujours les mêmes preuves en raison-
nant sur le même sentiment. Ses Ecrits s'expliquent alors les uns
par les autres, et les derniers, quand il a de la méthode, supposent
toujours les premiers. Voila ce que j'ai toujours tâché de faire, et
ce que j'ai fait, sur-tout, dans l'occasion dont il s'agit."

41 It is true that in a passage shortly preceding the "Profession
of Faith" Rousseau presents in his own name the doctrine of the
incompatibility between thought and matter. But in an earlier
version (Favre MS.) of this same passage he had presented *both*
sides of this question (i.e., also the position that thought is an
attribute of matter), and then concluded: "Je n'éxamine point
comment s'y prennent les philosophes pour resoudre cette ques-

tion. Ce n'est pas de cela qu'il s'agit ici; je veux seulement montrer quelle route immense a dû faire l'esprit humain simplement pour l'entendre et se la proposer, route d'autant plus abstruse et moins naturelle qu'elle est purement spéculative et bien loin de celle où nous mène la necessité de pourvoir à nos besoins qui est la route naturelle de l'instruction." Since this same intention clearly governs Rousseau's discussion of the two substances in the final version as well, it would be imprudent to regard the espousal of dualism there as definitive. The change from the earlier version may have been intended to remove a too obvious discrepancy between Rousseau and the vicar. Cf. *Emile*, P, 4:553 and *Emile (Manuscrit Favre)*, P, 4:217–20.

[42] *Emile*, P, 4:606.

[43] Ibid., P, 4:589–90.

[44] Ibid., P, 4:537.

[45] Plato, *Republic*, 608d–12a.

[46] Descartes, *Discourse on Method*, Fifth Part, last paragraph: ". . . après l'erreur de ceux qui nient Dieu . . . il n'y en a point qui éloigne plutôt les esprits faibles du droit chemin de la vertu que d'imaginer que l'âme des bêtes de même nature que la nôtre, et que par conséquent nous n'avons rien à craindre ni à espérer après cette vie, non plus que les mouches et les fourmis; au lieu que, lorsqu'on sait combien elles diffèrent, on comprend beaucoup mieux les raisons qui prouvent que la nôtre est d'une nature entièrement indépendante du corps, et par conséquent qu'elle n'est point sujette à mourir avec lui; puis, d'autant, qu'on ne voit point d'autres causes qui la détruisent, on est naturellement porté a juger de là qu'elle est immortelle."

[47] *Confessions*, P, 1:407.

[48] *Contract social* 4, chap. 8 [P, 3:468].

[49] Cf. *Contract social* 4, chap. 8 (note) [P, 3:468]: "Cesar plaidant pour Catalina tachoit d'établir le dogme de la mortalité de l'âme; Caton et Ciceron pour le réfuter ne s'amuserent point à philosopher; ils se contenterent de montrer que Cesar parloit en

mauvais Citoyen et avançoit une doctrine pernicieuse à l'Etat. En effet voilà dequoi devoit juger le Sénat de Rome, et non d'une question de théologie."

50 Castillon, *Discours sur l'origine*, pp. 43–44.

51 *Emile*, P, 4:586.

52 *Second Discourse*, p. 114 [P, 3:142].

53 See especially Note J, where Rousseau engages in an extensive discussion of the differences between men and animals without any mention of liberty, and refers unambiguously to "the faculty of perfecting itself, *which is the specific characteristic of the human species*" (italics mine, p. 208 [P, 3:211]).

54 Ibid., p. 97 [P, 3:127].

55 Ibid., p. 127 [P, 3:152]. Castillon (*Discours sur l'origine*, pp. 99–100) finds such a view incompatible with sound theology: "Ce Créateur nous auroit-il prodigué ses dons, s'ils eussent dû nous être inutiles pendant plusieurs siècles? Que servoit l'entendement aux hommes, pendant qu'ils ne raisonnoient pas? Quel avantage tiroient-ils de leur liberté, lorsqu'il n'avoient rien à choisir? Quelle utilité des organes de la parole, quand ils n'avoient point de langage? Quel fruit de la perfectibilité, dans le temps qu'ils étoient hors d'état de se perfectionner? Quel usage faisoient-ils de la commiseration lorsqu'ils vivoient dispersés dans les bois? ou des vertus sociales, lorsqu'ils n'avoient aucune société?"

56 *Second Discourse*, p. 140 [P, 3:162] (italics mine). This is clearly a well-considered statement on Rousseau's part. Cf. Ibid., p. 112 [P, 3:140], and *Lettre à Philopolis*, P, 3:232.

57 Robert Derathé, in his *Le rationalisme de J.-J. Rousseau* (Paris: Presses Universitaires de France, 1948), pp. 9–20, accepts at face value the doctrine of faculties belonging to man *"en puissance,"* but he recognizes the difficulty cited here, and the problem that it creates for his interpretation: "Le passage de l'état de nature à l'état civil, ou si l'on veut de la vie purement instinctive à la vie rationelle, reste la partie la plus faible du système de Rousseau. Car peut-on en même temps affirmer, comme le fait Rousseau, que l'homme est

sociable et raisonnable par nature, et faire dépendre le développement de la raison et de la sociabilité de simple 'accidents de la
nature,' de 'concours singuliers et fortuits de circonstances, qui
pouvaient fort bien ne jamais arriver'? Si c'est 'la raison qui fait
l'homme' elle doit se développer d'elle-même en vertu d'une néces-
sité interne, sans quoi l'humanité risquerait de ne pas réaliser les
virtualités fondamentales de sa nature, et par conséquent de man-
quer sa destination" (pp. 19–20).

58 *Second Discourse*, p. 126 [P, 3:151].

59 Ibid., p. 105 [P, 3:134].

60 Castillon, *Discours sur l'origine*, p. 35.

61 Cf. Ibid., p. 97: ". . . Ils [les hommes] ont toujours exercé les
facultés qu'ils tiennent de la nature. Le sens de ce mot dans cette
occasion en est une preuve evident."

62 *Second Discourse*, p. 115 [P, 3:142].

63 Ibid., p. 137 [P, 3:160].

64 Ibid., Note J, p. 204 [P, 3:208] (italics mine).

65 Ibid., p. 140 [P, 3:162].

66 Philopolis, *Lettre à Rousseau* (25 August 1755), reproduced
in the Pléiade Edition of Rousseau, 3:230 (note 1) (italics in the
original).

67 *Lettre à Philopolis*, P, 3:232.

68 Cf. Castillon, *Discours sur l'origine*, p. xvii: "Aussi pour tirer
l'homme de son prétendu état primitif a-t-on eu recours à des circonstances qui pouvaient ne pas arriver. Il a même fallu les fortifier
ces circonstances par la succession de plusieurs siècles. On avoue
donc que c'est par accident que nous sommes ce que nous sommes,
que c'est sans raison que la nature nous a donné des facultés inutile
sans la société. On nie donc le fameux axiôme que la nature ne fait
rien en vain."

69 Cf. Locke, *Essay Concerning Human Understanding*, Book
2, chapter 21, sec. 20:

"The attributing to faculties that which belonged not to them, has given occasion to this way of talking: but the introducing into discourses concerning the mind, with the name of faculties, a notion of *their* operating, has, I suppose, as little advanced our knowledge in that part of ourselves, as the great use and mention of the like invention of faculties, in the operations of the body, has helped us in the knowledge of physic. Not that I deny there are faculties, both in the body and mind: they both of them have their powers of operating, else neither the one nor the other could operate. For nothing can operate that is not able to operate; and that is not able to operate that has no power to operate. Nor do I deny that those words, and the like, are to have their place in the common use of languages that have made them current. It looks like too much affectation wholly to lay them by: and philosophy itself, though it likes not a gaudy dress, yet, when it appears in public, must have so much complacency as to be clothed in the ordinary fashion and language of the country, so far as it can consist with truth and perspicuity. But the fault has been, that faculties have been spoken of and represented as so many distinct agents. For, it being asked, what it was that digested the meat in our stomachs? it was a ready and very satisfactory answer to say that it was the *digestive faculty.* What was it that made anything come out of the body? the *expulsive faculty.* What moved? the *motive faculty.* And so in the mind, the *intellectual faculty,* or the understanding, understood; and the *elective* faculty, or the will, willed or commanded. This is, in short, to say, that the ability to digest, digested; and the ability to move, moved; and the ability to understand, understood. For faculty, ability, and power, I think, are but different names of the same things; which ways of speaking, when put into more intelligible words, will, I think, amount to thus much;—That digestion is performed by something that is able to digest, motion by something able to move, and understanding by something able to understand" (italics in the original).

[70] *Second Discourse*, p. 115 [P, 3:142].

[71] Ibid., Note J, p. 207 [P, 3:210].

[72] Cf. Castillon, *Discours sur l'origine*, p. 95:

"Il falloit montrer l'origine des inégalités qui accompagnent la société et on considere un être, qui en est incapable. Pour le

rendre propre a cet état, il a fallu le faire observer, inventer, ap-
perçevoir des rapports, connoître son coeur et celui de ses sem-
blables, forger une langue, enfin devenir homme.

"DEVENIR HOMME! Eh! s'écrient nos premiers pères avec
indignation, nous l'avons toujours été. . . ."

4

Morals

THE ANALYSIS OF ROUSSEAU'S DESCRIPTION of natural man from the metaphysical side has revealed that, for Rousseau, natural man is fundamentally an animal like any other. This view has obvious implications in regard to the moral character of natural man. Insofar as morality is properly understood as something specifically human, it would appear that Rousseau's natural man would be totally amoral—in other words, he would have no moral side at all. In fact, Rousseau draws just this conclusion:

> It seems at first that men in that state [the state of nature], not having among themselves any kind of moral relationship or known duties, could be neither good nor evil, and had neither vices nor virtues: unless, taking these words in a physical sense, one calls vices in the individual the qualities that can harm his own preservation, and virtues those that can contribute to it.[1]

Yet, as everyone knows, Rousseau is *the* philosopher who asserts that man is naturally good. In his *Letter to Beaumont* he states, "The fundamental principle of all morality, on the basis of which I have reasoned in all my writings . . . is that man is a being who is naturally good. . . ."² And in the *Second Discourse* itself Rousseau claims to have "demonstrated" this principle of man's natural goodness.³ The chief task facing the interpreter, then, must be to reconcile these two seemingly contradictory teachings—that man is naturally amoral and that man is naturally good.

First, it is necessary to make clear what Rousseau manifestly does *not* mean when he says that man is naturally good. He does not mean that men are naturally impelled to act benevolently toward their fellowmen. From the very outset of the *Second Discourse* he forthrightly rejects the principle of natural human sociability,⁴ and he makes it perfectly clear that the dominant motivation of natural man is self-love (*amour de soi*).⁵ Nor is Rousseau's natural man good in the sense that his passions are restrained by his reason or by his obedience to any law, for he is wholly lacking in reason and hence wholly governed by his passions. Rousseau spurns the entire classical tradition of moral and political philosophy which characterized man as a rational and sociable (or political) being. In so doing he aligns himself with a more recent tradition in moral and political philosophy whose two most conspicuous and infamous members were Hobbes and Mandeville. Rousseau himself indicates that he supports Hobbes's break with the earlier tradition by declaring that "Hobbes saw very clearly the defect of all modern definitions of natural right."⁶ And the extent of Rousseau's agreement with Mandeville is emphasized by Adam Smith, in a review of the *Second Discourse* for the British public:

> It is by the help of this style, together with a little philosophical chemistry, that the principles and ideas of the profligate Mandeville seem in him [i.e., Rousseau] to have all the purity and sublimity of the morals of Plato, and to be only the true spirit of a Republican carried a little too far.⁷

In asserting that Rousseau presents merely a slightly embellished and higher-toned version of the principles of Mandeville, Smith himself appears to have been carried a little too far. Yet his statement usefully and strikingly calls attention to the curious pedigree of Rousseau's moral teaching. The philosopher who most forcibly asserts man's natural goodness sides on certain critical questions with those philosophers who take the lowest view of man's nature—including even Mandeville, whom Rousseau himself calls "the most excessive detractor of human virtues."[8] Rousseau follows Mandeville and Hobbes (who is really the more crucial figure in this context) in denying that man is naturally sociable and that his reason can govern his passions; he agrees with them that man's "first care" is that of his preservation. In fact, it is precisely by taking Hobbes's principles (that man is naturally unsociable and governed principally by his desire for self-preservation) as his starting point that Rousseau arrives at what seem to be diametrically opposed conclusions. To understand Rousseau's moral teaching and especially his assertion that man is naturally good, one must begin by investigating his critique of Hobbes.

The Critique of Hobbes's State of Nature

Hobbes had described the state of nature, or the condition of men living outside of civil society, as a state of war—a war "of every man, against every man."[9] He cites three causes of quarrel that provoke this universal strife: competition, diffidence (i.e., fear), and glory (i.e., pride).[10] Rousseau attempts to refute Hobbes by showing that the state of nature is a peaceful condition for man. Hence he must show that the causes of war cited by Hobbes do not exist—or at least do not have the force that Hobbes ascribed to them—in the state of nature.

I. Competition

Competition, according to Hobbes, leads to war because "if any two men desire the same thing, which nevertheless they cannot both enjoy, they become enemies; and in the way to their end, which is principally their own conservation, and sometimes their delectation only, endeavour to destroy, or subdue one another."[11] In other words, there is a natural scarcity of the things men desire for the sake of their self-preservation. Rousseau counters this characterization of man's natural condition first of all by arguing that the state of nature is a state of plenty. He asserts that the earth is naturally fertile, and even devotes a note to a scientific proof of this proposition.[12] He further argues that man, because he is able to eat diverse kinds of food (i.e., both meat and vegetation), finds nourishment more easily than any other species.[13]

Yet posed only in these terms, the disagreement between Hobbes and Rousseau is perhaps not so great as it appears at first sight. The example that Hobbes gives of men's desiring the same thing is that "if one plant, sow, build, or possess a convenient seat, others may probably be expected to come prepared with forces united, to dispossess, and deprive him, not only of the fruit of his labour, but also of his life, or liberty."[14] Similarly, Rousseau, momentarily granting the supposition that man in the state of nature might have acquired the art of agriculture, asks, ". . . [W]hat man would be insane enough to torment himself cultivating a field that will be plundered by the first comer, whether man or beast, for whom the crop is suitable?"[15] But unlike Hobbes, Rousseau does not suppose that the cultivation of the earth is necessary to provide natural man with sufficient food to satisfy his desires. Yet this is not so much because Rousseau believes the earth is naturally more fertile than Hobbes had thought; it is rather because Rousseau believes the desires of natural man are much more modest than Hobbes had thought. In fact, in Note I of the *Second Discourse* Rousseau indicates that man in his primitive state nourished himself on "grass and acorns" (*d'herbe et de gland*).[16] Rousseau's real disagreement with Hobbes here is not about how generously the earth provides man with grass and acorns, but rather about whether men who live on such a diet can be contented.

Rousseau's state of nature differs from that of Hobbes, then, because Rousseau takes a different view about the passions that are natural to man. In the *Second Discourse* he says of natural man that "his desires do not exceed his physical needs"[17]—and *these* needs nature itself readily meets. Natural man desires food, not any particular kinds of food. His sense of taste is extremely crude.[18] Therefore, he has no need of agriculture, which "does not serve so much to bring forth from the earth foods it would easily provide without agriculture, as to force from it those preferences most to our taste."[19]

More generally, if natural man's desires are limited to simple physical necessities, then the conditions of the state of nature would not put men into competition with each other. In human terms, scarcity is not something absolute; it exists only in relation to our desires. For the most part, therefore, it becomes operative only insofar as our desires are articulated into preferences. Rousseau makes the same argument in regard to sex as he makes in regard to food. It is only the refined and particularized desires of civilized men that make sex into an object of competition. For men in the state of nature, one woman is as good as another.[20]

II. Diffidence

Since Hobbes presents diffidence, or fear of other men, as a natural outgrowth of competition, it could be contended that the Rousseauan arguments already cited are sufficient to dispose of this second cause of war. Because men are able to satisfy their natural desires by themselves, their interests do not conflict and they have no need of one another; hence, they would have no reason to fear one another. But Rousseau also adduces other powerful arguments that point to the absence of diffidence as a cause of war in the state of nature. For Hobbes, diffidence leads to war by prompting a man to "secure" himself by "anticipation . . . that is, by force, or wiles, to master the persons of all men he can, so long, till he sees no other power great enough to endanger him. . . ."[21] In acting by "anticipation," men are motivated by a concern for what may be called their long-range good. As Hobbes explains this behavior elsewhere, ". . . [T]he object of man's desire, is not to enjoy once only, and for one instant of time; but to assure for ever, the way of his future desire."[22] It is this human concern for the future that causes Hobbes to attribute to man "a perpetual and restless desire of power after power, that ceaseth only in death."[23]

Here again, Rousseau indicates that Hobbes endows natural man with a characteristic he could have acquired only after having left his primitive state. For Rousseau, natural man is "without any idea of the future, however near it may be, and his projects, as limited as his views, barely extend to the end of the day."[24] Without concern for his future good, man would be subject only to immediate fears—not to that "diffidence" which would predispose him to make war on other men. Moreover, natural man's total lack of foresight means that he is not even subject to that greatest of all fears, which Hobbes holds to be the decisive fact of the state of nature—namely, the fear of violent death.[25] For the knowledge of death, Rousseau argues, is another of those later acquisitions which man does not possess in his original state.[26]

III. Glory

Hobbes's third cause of quarrel, glory, is the only one that does not stem directly from man's natural desire for self-preservation. It leads men to use violence "for trifles, as a word, a smile, a different opinion, and any other sign of undervalue. . . ."[27] Once again, Rousseau argues that such considerations could not possibly move natural man. In Note O of the *Second Discourse*, he takes great pains to distinguish between the passion of self-love (*l'amour de soi-même*), which is "a natural sentiment which inclines every animal to watch over its own preservation," and the passion of vanity (*l'amour propre*), "a relative sentiment, artificial and born in society, which inclines each individual to have a greater esteem for himself than for anyone else." It is not possible for the latter to be present in natural man because it has "its source in comparisons he is not capable of making." On these same grounds, Rousseau goes on to argue that natural man is free of hate and of the desire for vengeance. Therefore, in the state of nature men

> . . . can do one another a great deal of mutual violence when they derive some advantage from it, without ever offending one another. In a word, every man, seeing his fellow-men hardly otherwise than he would see animals of another species, can carry off the prey of the weaker or relinquish his own to the stronger, without considering these plunderings as anything but natural events, without the slightest emotion of insolence or spite, and with no other passion than the sadness or joy of a good or bad outcome.[28]

This passage is striking in that Rousseau here appears to admit that in the state of nature competition on occasion leads men to commit violent acts toward one another. Yet this admission does not fundamentally weaken his argument that the state of nature is not a state of war. The reason for this may be stated as follows: Hobbes had emphasized that "War, consisteth not in battle only, or the act of fighting; but in a tract of time, wherein the will to contend by battle is sufficiently known. . . ."[29] And it is precisely this persisting "will to contend by battle" that Rousseau denies, partly because of other reasons that have already been indicated, but also because men have absolutely no concern for or interest in their fellowmen. Therefore, they regard an act of fighting as a purely natural and isolated event, one that produces in them no feelings about their opponents and creates no hostility that lasts beyond the fight itself. Men in the state of nature may wish to obtain an object which is held by one of their fellows, but (contrary to Hobbes's view) they never have "a desire and will to hurt,"[30] and therefore never enter a continuing state of enmity with other men.

There is clearly a common thread running through Rousseau's specific criticisms of the Hobbesian state of nature. Rousseau finds Hobbes's capital error in the fact that the latter "improperly included in the savage man's care of self-preservation the need to satisfy a multitude of passions which are the product of society and which have made laws necessary."[31] It is because Hobbes wrongly believed that certain artificial passions were natural to man that he misread the state of nature as a state of war.

The Sources of Our Knowledge of Natural Man

But it will not do simply to leave matters at that. To understand the deepest level of Rousseau's disagreement with Hobbes, it is necessary to examine the grounds on which each of these thinkers based his view of the passions natural to man and of the relations man naturally enjoys with his fellows. Hobbes uses two kinds of arguments to prove that the state of nature is a state of war. His basic approach is what he calls "inference made from the passions."[32] By beginning with the passions of men, one can deduce how men will behave in a situation where they are not held in check by a common power. But how does one learn which are the passions that govern men? Hobbes provides the answer in the introduction to *Leviathan*: "*Nosce teipsum, read thyself*," a saying meant "to teach us, that for the similitude of the thoughts and passions of one man, to the thoughts and passions of another, whosoever looketh into himself, and considereth what he doth, when he does *think*, *opine, reason, hope, fear,* &c, and upon what grounds; he shall thereby read and know, what are the thoughts and passions of all other men upon the like occasions."[33] The starting point for the inference from the passions is Hobbes's experience of his own passions.

For confirmation of the argument from the passions, Hobbes appeals to the experience of other men. He asks the skeptical reader to consider why, even in the midst of civil society, he locks his doors and his chests.[34] But more important, he calls attention to the actual conditions of men who live in a situation where they fear no common power: the savages in many parts of America and—the most decisive case of all—men living in times of civil war. And as a further example, he adduces the case of international relations, the warlike disposition of sovereign states toward one another.[35]

For Hobbes, then, the defining characteristic of the state of nature is simply the absence of a common power. An advanced society in the midst of a civil war is no less (and perhaps even more) in a state of nature than a primitive society of savages. In other words, the state of nature does not *essentially* antedate civil society. Hobbes even indicates that a state of nature may not in fact have always and everywhere preceded civil society: "It may peradventure be thought, there was never such a time, nor condition of war as this; and *I believe it was never so, over all the world.*"[36] This view seems to be in conflict with certain other aspects of Hobbes's teaching, especially his characterization of human speech as an *invention*, "without which, there had been amongst men, neither commonwealth, nor society, nor contract, nor peace, no more than amongst lions, bears, and wolves."[37] But whatever Hobbes's final views may have been about the origins and development of the human race, it is clear that his state of nature does not have an essentially historical dimension. For this reason he does not hesitate to derive his picture of the state of nature from his own experience and that of other civilized men—that is, to attribute to natural man the same passions as those of civil man.

Rousseau's criticism of Hobbes's procedure and therewith of Hobbes's state of nature is based on his own view of the essentially historical character of the state of nature.[38] Though he sometimes uses the term "state of nature" in only a juridical sense, to refer to the absence of legitimate government,[39] Rousseau identifies the "true" (*véritable*) state of nature with man's "original condition," or his "primitive state."[40] And this true state of nature, far from prompting men directly to the formation of civil society, is separated from it by an "immense space."[41] "The philosophers who have examined the foundations of society have all felt the necessity of going back to the state of nature, but none of them has reached it."[42] According to his own claim, it is Rousseau who for the first time gets all the way back to the origins and discovers the "forgotten and lost routes that must have led man from the natural state to the civil state."[43] The *Second Discourse* teaches man for the first time his true history.

According to Rousseau, then, the *true* state of nature cannot reemerge in civil war or other breakdowns of civil society. The history of mankind is not cyclical, it is progressive; it moves in one direction only. Even the savage peoples who can be observed have advanced far beyond their original condition. Everywhere the true state of nature seems already to have been transformed, and once it is transformed, it is irretrievably lost. But if the state of nature has, so to speak, disappeared, how can civilized man arrive at any knowledge about it? Rousseau's awareness of this problem is manifest at the very beginning of the *Second Discourse*. Though he, like Hobbes, begins by invoking the Delphic (and Socratic) injunction of *"Nosce teipsum,"* he immediately emphasizes the difficulty in applying this precept for men who are so far removed from their natural condition.[44] To overcome this difficulty he suggests a resort to scientific experiments that will enable one to make "solid observations" of natural man. But these experiments can be no more than a project for the future; the teaching of the *Second Discourse* therefore cannot possibly be based upon them.[45]

Rousseau does appeal to his observations of contemporary savage peoples to provide *some* confirmation of his view of the state of nature. Because they are closer to their original state, such savages are more natural than civilized men, and thus they help to reveal much of the artificiality of the civilized state. Yet there is much that is artificial even about those savage peoples whom Europeans have been able to observe. They have become vengeful and cruel, "while nothing is so gentle as a man in his primitive state."[46] They possess language and permanent families, neither of which belongs to man's original condition. Many essential aspects of the true state of nature, then, cannot be revealed by the evidence provided by savages. Therefore Rousseau supplements his observations of savage men with observations of other subjects—namely, beasts. The *Second Discourse*, more than any previous work of political philosophy, is filled with analogies and examples drawn from the animals. Evidence of what man's natural state is like is supplied by the conditions in which animals live.

Rousseau's Natural Man: Solitude and Stupidity

But the validity of this procedure is by no means self-evident, and Rousseau nowhere presents an explicit justification for his identification of man's "original condition" with "the animal condition."[47] Yet it is this identification that is at the very root of Rousseau's view of the state of nature, and hence its justification poses the essential problem of the *Second Discourse*. In the preceding chapter, this question was addressed in terms of Rousseau's metaphysics—his rejection of traditional views of man's origins in favor of the mechanistic account implied by modern science. But in the present context, this same issue can be approached from the "moral" side, by taking as a starting point Rousseau's critique of the Hobbesian view of natural man.

To recapitulate, Hobbes saw the state of nature as a state of war because he believed men's natural passions made them enemies of one another. Rousseau argues that the state of nature was a state of peace, not because men's passions were restrained by their reason, but because the scope of their passions was much narrower than Hobbes had thought. In the true state of nature, man's "desires do not exceed his [purely] physical needs," and are prompted only by "the simple impulsion of nature."[48] Now, Rousseau justifies the notion that man's natural desires are so extremely limited on the basis of two other features that he attributes to man in the state of nature—stupidity and solitude. Except for his purely physical needs, man can only desire that which he is capable of knowing; but since natural man is "deprived of every kind of enlightenment (*lumières*),"[49] he has only the simplest desires. Similarly, all those desires that go beyond men's necessities are "relative" desires, which arise from a concern with the opinions or actions of other men[50]; but since natural man has no relations with other men, he has no relative desires.

Hobbes had broken with the classical tradition of political philosophy by rejecting the traditional understanding of man as a rational animal and a political (or social) animal. He held instead that man's reason does not point toward the end or goal of human life, but is merely a means for helping to satisfy his passions ("For the thoughts are to the desires, as scouts, and spies, to range abroad, and find the way to the things desired. . . .")[51]; and that man is not naturally fit for society, because his concern for his own private good far outweighs any attachment he naturally has for other men.[52] What Rousseau does is to radicalize the grounds on which Hobbes broke with the classics: Not only is natural man not a being governed by reason, but he is totally lacking in reason; and not only is he an unsociable being, but he is completely solitary.

Men in the state of nature are solitary, according to Rousseau, because they are not brought together by mutual needs: "In fact, it is impossible to imagine why, in that primitive state, a man would sooner have need of another man than a monkey or a wolf of its fellow creature."[53] Having "neither harm to fear nor good to hope for"[54] from his fellows, natural man is much more radically self-sufficient and independent than Hobbes had believed him to be. Yet Rousseau goes further still, arguing not merely that men in the state of nature are totally independent of one another (i.e., that they are "morally" isolated from one another), but also that they are almost completely isolated from one another in a physical sense, that they "perhaps meet [one another] hardly twice in their lives."[55] It is only after they have already begun to progress beyond their primitive state that they begin to form troops similar to those formed by "crows or monkeys."[56] (This implies that men have even *less* need of their fellows than monkeys do.) Aristotle had asserted that "man is a political animal more than any bee or any other gregarious animal"[57]; Rousseau appears to hold that man is even more solitary than any asocial animal.

Why does Rousseau assert this extraordinary view, which is not supported by observations of any kind? The most plausible explanation seems to be that it is a conscious exaggeration employed for the following reason: By asserting that natural man is completely solitary, Rousseau is able to present a respectable defense of his account of man's natural stupidity.[58] The development of human reason depends upon language. But language, in turn, necessarily depends upon communication among men and could not develop without it. Therefore, if men naturally live in almost total isolation, they will be wholly lacking in reason and all the passions that depend upon reason. In this way, Rousseau is able to justify the brutish existence he attributes to natural man without seeming to take the shocking and heretical view that man possesses an essentially brutish nature.

Yet, as has been argued in chapter three, Rousseau does hold this latter view. Reason is not natural to man—not even "in potentiality." The crucial obstacle to man's acquisition of reason and language does not lie (as Rousseau's explicit emphasis seems to suggest) in men's physical isolation from one another. Even if men in their primitive state live in troops, as monkeys do, the essential problem remains: How can creatures to whom the ability to speak was in no way supplied by nature acquire speech? The decisive fact about natural man for Rousseau is not that he is *more solitary* than a monkey, but that he is *no more able to reason* than a monkey.[59] It is natural man's total lack of reason that is responsible for the moderate character of his desires: "Hobbes did not see that the same cause that prevents savages from using their reason, as our jurists claim, prevents them at the same time from abusing their faculties, as he himself claims."[60]

Hobbes had rejected the traditional definition of man as the rational animal along with the teleological view of the whole on which it was based. He had held that human reason has no support in the cosmic order and that human speech is an invention. According to the traditional view, man is most in harmony with nature when he exercises his reason. For Hobbes, man's use of reason sets him apart from nature and against nature; it helps him to overcome nature. On this issue Rousseau once again sides with Hobbes in rejecting the classical view. Yet it is precisely at this point that Rousseau makes his most profound and far-reaching criticism of Hobbes: Hobbes had not sufficiently reflected upon the *origins* of reason. Reason arises in man, but man is part of the natural order; he is an animal. If reason has no support in nature, it cannot belong to man in his natural condition. Man's original condition is that of an animal which possesses no greater share of reason than the other animals.

Precisely because man's natural condition is thus even more "brutish" than Hobbes had thought, Hobbes was wrong in viewing it as a condition of misery. It appears to be such only from the perspective of civil man, who has already acquired reason and a host of artificial desires. Viewed in its proper perspective, as a purely animal condition, it is a state of wholeness and self-sufficiency, and hence, one might say (and Rousseau sometimes does say), of a kind of goodness and happiness.[61] On occasion Rousseau asserts that man has been more favored by nature than the other animals; but at the very least, it may be said that men are as well equipped for survival as the other species, and are no more prone than they to fight among themselves.[62] Therefore, on the basis of his own principles, Hobbes should have concluded that the state of nature is "the best suited to peace and the most appropriate for the human race."[63] Consequently, the desire for their own preservation could not under ordinary circumstances have inspired men with the desire to depart from their natural state. Man's *natural* condition is a complete and harmonious one; civil society cannot be understood as its necessary consequence. It is only through a series of accidents that man arrives at an unstable and unsatisfactory situation which points toward civil society as its solution. It is only by accident that man is lifted out of animality and becomes a sociable being. And (as Rousseau writes elsewhere) "it is only in becoming sociable that he becomes a moral being, a rational animal, the king of the other animals, and the image of God on the earth."[64] In his natural, presocial condition, man simply is not a moral being, a rational animal, the king of the other animals, or the image of God on the earth.

Man's Natural Goodness

This points once again to the dilemma that was posed at the beginning of this chapter. Rousseau indeed holds at one and the same time that man is naturally amoral and that man is naturally good. Man is naturally good because he is totally innocent; he has no vices, because he has no knowledge of good and evil. The critic of *L'Année Littéraire* acutely seizes upon this implication of Rousseau's description of man's natural goodness, saying that "No one has ever doubted these truths, which signify nothing else than that in a state where man would be reduced to the condition of the beasts, he would not have the vices of a man."[65] Man's natural goodness is identical with animality. He is naturally good because he is "created" in the image, not of God, but of a beast.

The same critic goes on to draw out further consequences of the Rousseauan teaching:

> But in the state of nature, such as it is supposed [by Rousseau], if man did not have any vices, neither would he have had any virtues. He would have been deprived of liberty; for liberty implies preference, preference implies comparison, and comparison implies reasoning. But there is no reasoning in the state of nature, such as it is presented here: we would have been left to instinct alone—that is, to that sentiment excited by the needs of the body, which determines it to provide for them without delay: therefore there is no liberty, and consequently no morals and no virtues.[66]

Precisely because he never strays from his natural goodness, original man is incapable of morality. Goodness and virtue, far from being synonymous for Rousseau, are in conflict with each other.[67] Goodness comes directly from nature; virtue or morality is opposed to nature. Virtue exists only in relation to duties; it demands choice, and hence "moral liberty." Goodness, on the other hand, flows directly from the "simple impulsions of nature"; it obeys no duties or constraints. Goodness knows no law. Hence it goes together not with moral liberty but with "natural liberty"—that is, liberty understood merely as independence. In the state of nature, man enjoys his full natural liberty, but he is totally without moral liberty.[68] He is in complete harmony with nature; but viewed from a different perspective, this means that he is completely enslaved by physical (i.e., bodily) nature.

To further clarify this interpretation of Rousseau's doctrine of man's natural goodness, it will be helpful to examine an important passage in which Rousseau defends that doctrine before the ecclesiastical authorities in his *Letter to Beaumont*:

> The fundamental principle of all morality, on the basis of which I have reasoned in all my writings, and which I have developed in this most recent work [i.e., *Emile*] with all the clarity of which I was capable, is that man is a being that is naturally good, loving justice and order; that there is no original perversity in the human heart, and that the first motions of nature are always right. I have shown that the only passion that is born with man—namely, self-love (*l'amour de soi*)—is a passion indifferent in itself to good and evil; that it does not become good or bad except by accident and according to the different circumstances in which it develops. I have shown that all the vices that are imputed to the human heart are not natural to it; I have said in what manner they are born; I have, so to speak, followed their genealogy, and I have shown how, by the successive alterations of their natural goodness, men finally become what they are.
>
> I have further explained what I understood by this original goodness, which does not seem to follow (*se déduire*) from the indifference to good and evil natural to self-love. Man is not a simple being; he is composed of two substances. If everybody does not agree on this, you and I agree on it, and I have tried to prove it to others. Once this is proven, self-love is no longer a simple passion, but has two principles

—namely, the intelligent being and the sensitive being—whose well-being is not the same. The appetite of the senses tends to the well-being of the body, and the love of order to that of the soul. This latter love, developed and rendered active, is called the conscience. . . .[69]

In the first of these two paragraphs, Rousseau interprets natural goodness along the lines that have been suggested above (except for his one brief reference to man's "loving justice and order"): Man's only natural passion—self-love—is indifferent to good and evil, and takes on a moral cast only as a result of accident; therefore, no vices are natural to man. But at the beginning of the second paragraph, Rousseau offers another explanation of original goodness, which he now says "does not *seem* to follow from the indifference to good and evil natural to self-love." This second interpretation is based on the dualist metaphysics of the "Profession of Faith of a Savoyard Vicar." It assumes an innate principle of "intelligence" in man, a love of order that tends toward the well-being of the soul and that develops into the conscience.

But as has been shown in chapter three, the argument of the *Second Discourse* in no way rests on the dualist metaphysics of the Savoyard Vicar; it is, in fact, incompatible with many of the central principles set forth by the Vicar. In the *Second Discourse* Rousseau does not speak of an innate principle of intelligence, or of the well-being of the soul as distinct from that of the body. The natural man of the *Second Discourse* is in fact "a simple being."[70] Moreover, in the *Second Discourse* proper, there is not even a single mention of the conscience.[71] Consequently, it must be concluded that the argument for man's natural goodness that Rousseau claims to have "demonstrated" in the *Second Discourse* follows, not from any natural human "love of order," but precisely from "the indifference to good and evil natural to [the 'simple passion' of] self-love."

The passage quoted above from the *Letter to Beaumont* continues as follows:

> But the conscience only develops and acts with man's intelligence (*avec les lumières de l'homme*). It is only by his intelligence (*ces lumières*) that he arrives at knowledge of order, and it is only when he knows it that his conscience leads him to love it. Conscience therefore is nothing (*nulle*) in the man who has not compared anything, and who has not seen his relations. In this state man knows only himself; he does not see his well-being as something in opposition to or in conformity with the well-being of anyone else; he neither hates nor loves anything; limited to physical instinct alone, he is nothing (*nul*), he is a beast; this is what I have shown in my *Discourse on Inequality.*[72]

At the conclusion of this paragraph, Rousseau states straightforwardly the proposition that is at the core of the interpretation of the *Second Discourse* offered in this essay—namely, that in the state of nature man is "limited to physical instinct alone . . . he is a beast." Rousseau is able to affirm this conclusion so boldly here because of the context. He has just previously stated that a spiritual principle, the love of order, is part of man's nature. Therefore, his assertion that man is a beast seemingly applies only to a situation in which certain circumstances have prevented man from developing his spiritual faculties along the lines nature had intended. But according to this view, such a situation could not properly be understood as man's *natural* situation—even if it were man's *original* situation. In other words, such a view would point toward the classical orientation, according to which the primitive was understood not as that which is natural, but as that which is defective, incomplete, and hence unnatural. This is precisely the orientation which is expressed by the quote from Aristotle's *Politics* that appears on the title page of the *Second Discourse*: "*Non in depravatis, sed in his quae bene secundum naturam se habent, consideran-dum est quid sit naturale."*[73]

Yet the *Second Discourse* as a whole leaves no doubt that Rousseau stands this Aristotelian view on its head. From the very first paragraph of the Preface, it becomes clear that Rousseau identifies that which is natural and uncorrupted not with the fully developed, but with the primitive.[74] The primitive state described in the *Second Discourse* is also man's *natural* state. There are no "principles" that properly belong to man's nature and yet are completely inoperative in his original condition. If man is no more than a beast in his primitive state, it is because man's nature is simply no higher than that of the beasts.

Pity

In the *Second Discourse* Rousseau nowhere speaks of a separate "principle" in natural man that aims at the good of the soul as distinct from that of the body. But he does speak of a somewhat different kind of "principle" that exists alongside (bodily) self-love—pity, or "a natural repugnance to see any sensitive being perish or suffer, principally our fellowmen."[75] Rousseau concludes his explicit critique of Hobbes by pointing to the latter's failure to discern the role played by pity in the state of nature: Pity "softens" the desire for self-preservation[76]; this would constitute an additional reason why the state of nature is not a state of war. Moreover, to say that man is naturally compassionate implies that he has a natural concern for the well-being of his fellowmen, that he is not merely a self-regarding being. Pity seems to supply an additional dimension to man's natural goodness. Even more than that, it seems to lend some positive and human content to the notion of natural goodness, which heretofore has been interpreted as being wholly negative and brutish. Thus a full interpretation of the teaching of the *Second Discourse* about man's natural goodness must include an account of Rousseau's teaching about pity.

At the beginning of his discussion of pity in the First Part, Rousseau calls it a "natural virtue" (one that even Mandeville had been forced to recognize).[77] But as the discussion proceeds, Rousseau refers to pity not as a virtue, but as a "natural sentiment."[78] (This latter description is much more in accord with that offered in the Preface, where he speaks of the "inner impulsion of commiseration."[79]) Therefore, he is able to conclude that in the state of nature pity *"takes the place of laws, morals, and virtue."*[80] In fact, then, Rousseau agrees with Mandeville's own insistence that pity, though it may sometimes counterfeit virtue, is merely a passion.[81]

But being a passion, pity need not necessarily be something distinctively human. Indeed, Rousseau presents a number of examples of "perceptible signs" of pity found among the beasts.[82] Like self-love, pity is an attribute of other animals as well as of man. In itself, man's natural compassion does not distinguish him from or raise him above the beasts. Thus the anonymous critic of *L'Année Littéraire* can speak of the "two principles that he [Rousseau] regards as the only ones natural to man, because they are anterior to reason and they confound us with the beasts."[83]

Furthermore, these two natural passions, pity and self-love, are not of equal rank. Rousseau makes it clear that when they come into conflict—that is, where self-preservation is concerned—pity is legitimately overruled.[84] The conjunction of these two principles gives rise not to that "sublime maxim of reasoned justice," the Biblical injunction *"Do unto others as you would have them do unto you,"* but to "this other maxim of natural goodness . . . *Do what is good for yourself with the least possible harm to others."*[85] But what is the practical import of this latter maxim in the Rousseauan state of nature? For in the state of nature, it will be remembered, men have almost no relations with one another. Their needs do not bring them together, nor are they forced into a condition of mutual competition. They have no desire to do harm to their fellows. Therefore the restraint imposed by natural pity would seem to be superfluous. But even if, as Rousseau sometimes seems to admit, there occasionally does arise a situation in the state of nature where men commit mutual violence, it is only where their preservation is concerned.[86] And this is precisely the circumstance in which the impulse toward commiseration is rendered nugatory by the superior force of self-love. A being whose desires do not exceed his physical needs can hardly be checked in the fulfillment of those desires by the "gentle voice" of pity.[87]

Finally, a word must be said about the curious character of the arguments that Rousseau adduces in support of the naturalness of pity. The bulk of these arguments are based upon examples drawn from the behavior of men living not in the state of nature but in civil society. Thus, for instance, he compares the commiseration displayed by *"la canaille"* with the indifference to the plight of his fellows shown by the philosopher; philosophy, he asserts, "turns man back upon himself" and "isolates" him.[88] This passage seems to imply that the disposition of the philosopher is merely the artificial product of reason, while the sentiment of the populace is much more natural. Yet, however much the philosopher may differ from primitive man in other respects, is not the very hallmark of man in Rousseau's state of nature the kind of independence and self-sufficiency here attributed to the philosopher?

The other kind of evidence that Rousseau cites to defend the naturalness of pity is drawn from the behavior of beasts. He points, for example, to "the repugnance of horses to trample a living body underfoot."[89] The problem with this kind of analogy, however, is that, at best, it is insufficient to establish more than that men are as compassionate as horses. While it may indicate that men have certain instinctive reactions that can be seen as the root of compassion, it does not show that in the state of nature this produces a more general disposition toward compassionate behavior. This point may be clarified by reference to another kind of instinctive reaction that Rousseau admits may be attributable to men in the state of nature— namely, vengeance. For he states that "they did not even dream of vengeance, except perhaps mechanically and on the spot, like the dog that bites the stone thrown at him." [90] Although this example of instinctive vengeance seems exactly parallel to instinctive pity as demonstrated by the horse who avoids trampling upon a living body, Rousseau does *not* hold that man is naturally vengeful. For insofar as vengeance can be understood as having important consequences—that is, insofar as it can be understood as more than a momentary reaction—it must have "its source in comparisons he [natural man] is not capable of making." [91] Natural man is too stupid to be guided by vengeance. But then is he not also too stupid to be guided by pity?

In fact, this is exactly the view that Rousseau takes in his *Essay on the Origin of Language*, a work unpublished in Rousseau's lifetime, but written more or less contemporaneously with the *Second Discourse* [92]:

Pity, although natural to the human heart, would remain eternally inactive without the imagination, which puts it into play. How do we let ourselves be moved to pity? In transporting ourselves outside of ourselves; in identifying with the suffering being. We suffer only insofar as we judge that he suffers; it is not in ourselves, it is in him that we suffer. Think how much this transporting presupposes acquired knowledge. How would I imagine pains of which I had no idea? How would I suffer in seeing another suffer, if I did not even know that he was suffering, if I was unaware of what we had in common? He who has never reflected cannot be clement, or just, or compassionate; neither can he be wicked or vindictive. He who imagines nothing is aware (*sent*) only of himself; he is alone in the middle of the human race.[93]

Moreover, a careful reading of the *Emile* shows that this is also the view that Rousseau takes in this later work. For in the *Emile* Rousseau states: "The source of all our passions, the origin and principle of all the others, the only one which is born with man and does not leave him as long as he lives, is self-love (*l'amour de soi*); a passion that is primitive, innate, anterior to every other, and of which all the others are in a sense only modifications."[94] Pity, like vanity (*l'amour propre*), is born only when men begin to compare themselves with their fellows.[95]

Moreover, there is considerable evidence for this kind of interpretation in the *Second Discourse* itself, especially in the manner in which Rousseau links his discussion of pity with his discussion of vanity. For the very opening sentence of the section on pity in the First Part of the *Discourse* is also the sentence in which Rousseau first introduces the distinction between self-love and vanity: "There is, besides, another principle which Hobbes did not notice, and which—having been given to man in order to soften, under certain circumstances, the ferocity of his vanity or the desire for self-preservation before the birth of vanity (O)—tempers the ardor he has for his own well-being by an innate repugnance to see his fellow-man suffer."[96] In Note O, which is appended to this sentence, Rousseau elaborates upon the distinction between self-love ("a natural sentiment which inclines every animal to watch over its own preservation") and vanity ("a relative sentiment, artificial and born in society").[97] He attempts to show that vanity and the passions related to it (hate and the desire for vengeance) do not exist in the state of nature. But the arguments he uses (naural man's self-sufficiency and stupidity) would serve with equal force to show that *pity* does not exist in the state of nature. This note concludes as follows: "In a word, every man, seeing his fellowmen hardly otherwise than he would see animals of another species, can carry off the prey of the weaker or relinquish his own to the stronger, without considering these plunderings as anything but natural events, without the slightest emotion of insolence or spite, and with no other passion than the sadness or joy of a good or bad outcome."[98]

So much for natural pity. It must be concluded that pity "softens" not so much Rousseau's natural man as Rousseau's presentation of his natural man. Man's natural goodness lacks the human and positive aspect that we associate with genuine compassion. The only principle that truly governs man (or any other animal) in the state of nature is self-love. Thus man's natural goodness must indeed be wholly derived "from the indifference to good and evil natural to self-love."[99] Man is good in the state of nature because he is completely amoral. More than that, he is submoral and hence subhuman. He is merely another beast, just one more part of the blind mechanism of nature.

Notes

1 *Second Discourse*, p. 128 [P, 3:152].

2 *Lettre à Beaumont*, P, 4:935.

3 *Second Discourse*, Note I, p. 193 [P, 3:203].

4 Ibid., p. 95 [P, 3:126].

5 Ibid., pp. 95–96, 130; Note O, pp. 221–22 [P, 3:126, 154, 219].

6 Ibid., p. 129 [P, 3:153].

7 Adam Smith, in the *Edinburgh Review*, no. 1 (January–July 1755), pp. 74–75. Earlier in his review, Smith makes a similar remark about the *Second Discourse*: "Whoever reads this last work with attention will observe, that the second volume of the *Fable of the Bees* has given occasion to the system of M. Rousseau, in whom however the principles of the English author are softened, improved, and embellished, and stript of all that tendency to corruption and licentiousness which has disgraced them in their original author" (p. 73).

8 *Second Discourse*, p. 130 [P, 3:154].

9 Thomas Hobbes, *Leviathan*, ed., Michael Oakeshott (Oxford: Basil Blackwell, 1960), 1, chap. 13, p. 82.

10 Ibid., 1, chap. 13, p. 81.

11 Ibid., 1, chap. 13, p. 81.

12 *Second Discourse*, p. 105; Note D, pp. 186–87 [P, 3:135, 198].

13 Ibid., p. 106 [P, 3:135].

14 Hobbes, *Leviathan*, 1, chap. 13, p. 81.

15 *Second Discourse*, pp. 118–19 [P, 3:145].

16 Ibid., Note I, p. 202 [P, 3:207].

17 Ibid., p. 116; Note K, p. 213 [P, 3:143, 214].

18 Ibid., p. 113 [P, 3:140].

19 Ibid., p. 118 [P, 3:145].

20 Ibid., pp. 134–35 [P, 3:157–58].

21 Hobbes, *Leviathan*, 1, chap. 13, p. 81.

22 Ibid., 1, chap. 11, p. 63.

23 Ibid., 1, chap. 11, p. 64.

24 *Second Discourse*, p. 117 [P, 3:144].

25 Hobbes, *Leviathan*, 1, chap. 13, pp. 80, 82, 84; chap. 14, p. 85.

26 *Second Discourse*, p. 116 [P, 3:143].

27 Hobbes, *Leviathan*, 1, chap. 13, p. 82.

28 *Second Discourse*, Note O, pp. 221–22 [P, 3:219–20].

29 Hobbes, *Leviathan*, 1, chap. 13, p. 82.

30 Thomas Hobbes, *De Cive, or the Citizen*, ed. Sterling P. Lamprecht (New York: Appleton-Century-Crofts, 1949), 1, chap. 4, p. 25.

31 *Second Discourse*, p. 129 [P, 3:153].

32 Hobbes, *Leviathan*, 1, chap. 13, p. 82.

33 Ibid., Introduction, p. 6.

34 Ibid., 1, chap. 13, p. 82.

35 Ibid., 1, chap. 13, p. 83.

36 Ibid., 1, chap. 13, p. 83 (italics mine).

37 Ibid., 1, chap. 4, p. 18.

38 Cf. Roger Masters, *The Political Philosophy of Rousseau*, (Princeton: Princeton University Press, 1968) pp. 198–99 and Note 175.

39 Further discussion of this purely juridical use of the term by Rousseau will be found in the next chapter. See below, pp. 99–101.

40 See especially *Second Discourse*, Note O, p. 222 [P, 3:219].

41 Ibid., p. 178 [P, 3:192].

[42] Ibid., p. 102 [P, 3:132].

[43] Ibid., p. 178 [P, 3:191].

[44] Ibid., p. 91 [P, 3:122]. Later in the Preface, it is true, Rousseau at one point claims to proceed by "meditating on the first and simplest operations of the human soul" (p. 95). This at first sight seems to suggest that Rousseau's view of natural man is ultimately founded upon introspection—in other words, that he follows the same procedure as Hobbes, only he believes to read himself more profoundly than Hobbes had done. Yet such an introspective approach is not invoked elsewhere in the *Discourse*, and in any case, it is not clear how it could surmount the epistemological problem that Rousseau himself raises. Rousseau indeed meditates *on* "the first and simplest operations of the human soul," but he discovers which operations these are not by introspection but by reasoning about man's place in the natural order.

[45] Ibid., p. 93 [P, 3:123–24].

[46] Ibid., pp. 149–50 [P, 3:170].

[47] Ibid., p. 116 [P, 3:143]; see also Note L, p. 219 [P, 3:217].

[48] Ibid., p. 116 [P, 3:143].

[49] Ibid., p. 116 [P, 3:143].

[50] Ibid., Note O, p. 222 [P, 3:219].

[51] Hobbes, *Leviathan*, 1, chap. 8, p. 46.

[52] Hobbes, *De Cive*, 1, chap. 2, pp. 21–24.

[53] *Second Discourse*, p. 126 [P, 3:151].

[54] Ibid., p. 128 [P, 3:153].

[55] Ibid., p. 119 [P, 3:146].

[56] Ibid., p. 145 [P, 3:167].

[57] Aristotle, *Politics*, 1253a7–9.

[58] Cf. Masters, *Political Philosophy of Rousseau*, pp. 135–36.

[59] For this reason, arguments that use evidence drawn from the behavior of subhuman primates to refute Rousseau's account of

the asocial character of natural man have already conceded his fundamental premise: that man does not essentially differ from the brutes. And once this point has been conceded, no amount of evidence attesting to the complex "social" structure among baboons can possibly restore the traditional view of man as a social or political animal. For the traditional notion of man as a social animal is inextricably tied to the view that man is the rational animal. This is not to deny, however, that evidence of hierarchical relationships within bands of primates may prove fatal to Rousseau's contention that natural man lacks all traces of *amour-propre*.

[60] *Second Discourse*, p. 129 [P, 3:154].

[61] Ibid., pp. 115, 127; Note I, pp. 192–93 [P, 3:142, 152, 202].

[62] Ibid., pp. 105–13, 136–37 [P, 3:135–41, 159].

[63] Ibid., p. 129 [P, 3:153].

[64] *Fragments Politiques*, P, 3:477.

[65] *L'Année Littéraire* vol. 7, Lettre 7 (n.p., 1755), p. 157. Cf. Jean de Castillon, *Discours sur l'origine de l'inégalité parmi les hommes—pour servir de réponse au Discours que M. Rousseau, Citoyen de Genève, a publié sur le même sujet* (Amsterdam, 1756), pp. 131–32: "Cependant, si l'on en croit Rousseau, naturellement l'homme n'est ni vicieux ni sociable. Non, il ne l'est point pendant qu'il est brute; mais il l'est, lorsqu'il est l'homme."

[66] *L'Année Littéraire* 7 (1755): 157.

[67] Cf. *Rousseau Juge de Jean-Jacques*, P, 1:670, 823; *Reveries d'un Promeneur Solitaire*, P, 1:1052–53.

[68] For a further discussion of Rousseau's understanding of liberty, see below, pp. 112–15.

[69] *Lettre à Beaumont*, P, 4:935–36.

[70] Consider the reference to natural man as a being "acting always by fixed and invariable principles," and possessing a "heavenly and majestic *simplicity* with which its author had endowed it." *Second Discourse*, p. 91 [P, 3:122] (italics mine).

[71] There is one such mention in the Dedication. Ibid., p. 85 [P, 3:116].

⁷² *Lettre à Beaumont*, P, 4:936.

⁷³ *Second Discourse*, p. 77 [P, 3:109]: "Not in corrupt things, but in those which are well ordered in accordance with nature, should one consider that which is natural" (Aristotle, *Politics*, 1254a36–38).

⁷⁴ *Second Discourse*, p. 91 [P, 3:122].

⁷⁵ Ibid., p. 95 [P, 3:126].

⁷⁶ Ibid., p. 130 [P, 3:154].

⁷⁷ Ibid., p. 130 [P, 3:154].

⁷⁸ Ibid., pp. 132–33 [P, 3:156].

⁷⁹ Ibid., p. 96 [P, 3:126].

⁸⁰ Ibid., p. 133 [P, 3:156] (italics mine).

⁸¹ Mandeville, "An Essay on Charity and Charity-Schools," in *The Fable of the Bees*, ed. Phillip Harth (Baltimore: Penguin Books, 1970), pp. 264–69.

⁸² *Second Discourse*, p. 130 [P, 3:154].

⁸³ *L'Année Littéraire* 7 (1755): 151.

⁸⁴ *Second Discourse*, pp. 96, 133 [P, 3:126, 156].

⁸⁵ Ibid., p. 133 [P, 3:156] (italics in original).

⁸⁶ Ibid., pp. 133–34; Note I, p. 195; Note O, p. 222 [P, 3:157, 203, 219–20].

⁸⁷ Ibid., p. 133 [P, 3:156].

⁸⁸ Ibid., p. 132 [P, 3:156].

⁸⁹ Ibid., p. 130 [P, 3:154].

⁹⁰ Ibid., p. 134 [P, 3:157].

⁹¹ Ibid., Note O, p. 222 [P, 3:219].

⁹² See P, 1:560 (note 3) on the controversy surrounding the date of composition of the *Essai sur l'origine des langues*.

⁹³ *Essai sur l'origine des langues*, 9, second paragraph.

Notes

[94] *Emile*, P, 4:491.

[95] Cf. Masters, *Political Philosophy of Rousseau*, pp. 136–46. Though Masters follows a similar line of argument in concluding that pity is not operative in the state of nature, he holds to the view that pity is natural to man and a decisive element of his natural goodness.

[96] *Second Discourse*, p. 130 [P, 3:154].

[97] Ibid., Note O, pp. 221–22 [P, 3:219–20].

[98] Ibid., Note O, p. 222 [P, 3:219–20].

[99] *Lettre à Beaumont*, quoted above, p. 79.

5

Politics

THE INTRODUCTORY CHAPTER of this essay emphasized the apparent divergence between Rousseau's teaching about the state of nature and the political teaching that he adumbrates in the *Second Discourse* and develops in the *Social Contract*.[1] The conclusions reached in the succeeding chapters serve only to sharpen the problem: If man by nature is merely a beast, lacking any moral dimension, where can valid principles that might serve as a guide for political life possibly be found? An analysis of the Rousseauan state of nature cannot be considered complete unless it attempts to identify the links between Rousseau's natural science and his political science. The central question that remains to be addressed may be posed as follows: How can "the study of original man" provide—in accordance with Rousseau's claim in the Preface to the *Second Discourse*—any insight into "the true foundations of the body politic, [and] the reciprocal rights of its members"?[2]

As in regard to morality, so also in regard to politics, the Rousseauan state of nature first of all has certain crucial negative implications. Rousseau is led to present an account of the

[*95*]

state of nature in the course of an inquiry into "the Origin and Foundations of Inequality Among Men." From a political point of view, there is one sort of inequality that is decisive—the inequality between rulers and ruled, between those who command and those who obey. In regard to this fundamental area of inequality, the teaching of the *Second Discourse* is clear: It has no foundation whatsoever in nature. Or, as Rousseau succinctly states in the *Social Contract*, ". . . no man has a natural authority over his fellowmen."[3] This argument is hardly an original one on Rousseau's part. Diderot's article on "Political Authority" in the first volume of the *Encyclopedia* (which appeared in 1751, four years before the publication of the *Second Discourse*) begins with the words: "No man has received from nature the right of commanding others."[4] This premise is stated with almost equal explicitness by both Hobbes and Locke.[5] Indeed, it might be said that the very notion of the "state of nature" in modern political philosophy was from its inception bound up with the denial of a natural right to rule.

But to say that this view was not original to Rousseau is in no way to say that it was not controversial. In fact, Diderot's article on "Political Authority"—a work much more moderate than the *Second Discourse*—created an uproar that led to the censoring of the *Encyclopedia* by the royal authorities. And in the "Errata" that accompanied the appearance of the third volume of the *Encyclopedia* in 1753, the authors took pains to acknowledge that "the authority of legitimate princes comes from God."[6] The doctrine of divine right, from which Rousseau explicitly abstracts in the *Second Discourse*,[7] and the doctrines that supported political authority by reference to paternal power or the law of the stronger (*le droit du plus fort*), which he attempts to refute in both the *Second Discourse* and the *Social Contract*,[8] were very much alive in eighteenth-century Europe. The effort to explode these doctrines is an important part of Rousseau's intention in the *Second Discourse*, and cannot be ignored in an assessment of the political implications of the Rousseauan state of nature.

Rousseau's attack, however, is directed not only against the defenders of absolute monarchy but also against the whole classical tradition of political philosophy, and especially its most prominent representative, Aristotle. In this context, it is once again instructive to look at the quote from Aristotle's *Politics* that serves as the epigraph to the *Second Discourse*: "*Non in depravatis, sed in his quae bene secundum naturam se habent, considerandum est quid sit naturale.*" In the *Politics* this statement occurs right at the heart of the argument in favor of natural slavery. Aristotle proceeds by arguing that hierarchical organization, or a principle of ruling and subordination, is characteristic of all living things and of nature as a whole. The two crucial examples that he cites of such a natural hierarchy are the rule of the soul over the body and the rule of intellect (*nous*) or reason over the passions. In those men who are not corrupt, but maintain themselves according to nature, the soul will rule the body and reason will rule the passions. Therefore men in whom the soul and the intellect govern by nature have a title to rule those men who are governed by the body and by the passions.[9]

Here again, Rousseau turns the Aristotelian teaching on its head. The *Second Discourse* teaches that the satisfaction of his bodily needs is the sole concern of natural man, and that, far from governing his passions by his intellect, natural man does not even possess reason. Hence the political consequences that Rousseau derives from his consideration of natural man are wholly antithetical to Aristotle's conclusion that some men have a natural right to rule over others.[10] Rousseau's study of man in his natural state shows that all men are by nature concerned above all with the preservation of their bodies and the satisfaction of their passions, and that they therefore are naturally equal.

Because men are naturally equal in this way, they are also naturally free. In the state of nature no man can enjoy a superiority in wisdom (i.e., reason) that would entitle him to decide what is best for another. Since all men are equally subject to the "law" that compels them to look after their self-preservation, each man "himself alone being the judge of the means to preserve himself thereby becomes his own master."[11] As no man has any natural obligation to let himself be guided by another in any matter whatsoever, all men enjoy a perfect liberty vis-à-vis one another.

All men are born free and equal, yet they live in civil societies that are characterized by inequality, or the subjection of some men to the authority of others. That authority cannot come from nature; it therefore must either be wholly without foundation or it must rest on some foundation other than nature. The *Second Discourse* and the *Social Contract* are both attempts, from somewhat different points of view, to find such an extranatural foundation for political authority. The answer to this problem that is proposed by both works is the same: Political authority, insofar as it is not wholly without foundation—that is, illegitimate—must be based on the agreement of those subject to that authority. Men who are naturally free and equal cannot owe any obligation to other men unless that obligation is created by their own consent. The only possible foundation for the right to exercise political rule is an agreement or contract on the part of those involved.

The consequence of this view is that wherever political authority that is not founded upon such a contract is exercised and enforced, this is done without right and hence is indistinguishable from mere violence. "The uprising that ends by strangling or dethroning a sultan is as lawful (*juridique*) an act as those by which he disposed, the day before, of the lives and goods of his subjects. Force alone maintained him, force alone overthrows him. Everything thus occurs according to the natural order. . . ." [12] The deterioration of legitimate government into despotism, Rousseau asserts, brings about a "new state of nature." [13]

The Two Meanings of the "State of Nature"

By calling despotism a new state of nature, Rousseau here seems to accept the Hobbesian notion according to which a state of nature may reemerge in the midst of civil society. The state of nature persists as long as it is not overcome by the establishment of a body politic; therefore, the dissolution of the contract upon which the body politic is founded restores the state of nature. It is true, of course, that Rousseau does not follow Hobbes in defining the state of nature simply by the absence of a common power. He accepts Locke's correction of Hobbes—namely, the denial that *despotical* power can be based upon a contract [14]—and defines the state of nature by the absence of *legitimate* power. Yet this does not alter the fact that the state of nature, when defined in this manner, loses its essentially historical character.

Although the preceding chapters of this essay have emphasized the essential historicity of the Rousseauan state of nature, it now must be acknowledged that this concept has a *dual aspect* in the *Second Discourse*. More precisely, Rousseau uses the term "state of nature" in two different senses, a *historical* sense and a *juridical* sense. The first identifies the state of nature as the original condition of the human race; the second identifies it as any condition of men who do not live under legitimate government.

One way of reconciling these two differing concepts of the state of nature would be to say that the second is the more fundamental, on the grounds that it seems more comprehensive than the first: The state of nature understood as the absence of legitimate government also embraces man's original condition, where there is no government at all. Rousseau refers to the time

between the establishment of landed property and the establishment of laws as the "last stage of the state of nature."[15]
Similarly, man's original condition could be considered merely
the first stage of the state of nature. Indeed, Rousseau sometimes refers to it as the "*primitive* state of nature" or the "*first*
state of nature."[16] From this perspective, the different stages
of progress within the state of nature would be of no fundamental significance. The only crucial instance of "progress"
would be that whose identification Rousseau says (in the Introduction) is the chief task of the *Second Discourse*: "the moment
when, right taking the place of violence, nature was subjected
to law. . . ."[17] And if this is the decisive moment, one must conclude that the decisive opposition or dichotomy of the *Second
Discourse* is that between the state of nature on the one hand,
and (legitimate) political society on the other.

Yet this interpretation is open to powerful objections. The
analysis in the preceding chapters of the metaphysical and
moral teachings of the *Second Discourse* has demonstrated the
crucial importance of the historical dimension of Rousseau's
state of nature.[18] Here it suffices to point out that Rousseau
refers to man's original condition not merely as the "first" or
"primitive" state of nature, but also as the "*pure (pur)* state
of nature," and even more significantly, as the "*true (véritable)*
state of nature."[19] On the basis of this evidence, one might conclude that, strictly speaking, the term "state of nature" may
properly be applied only to man's original condition; the juridical application of the term to an era in which men have
already departed from their original condition would thus be
merely a loose usage. Rousseau identifies the true state of
nature with a "state of animality," which is a state of independence and stupidity.[20] From this point of view, then, the
decisive opposition of the *Second Discourse* would be that between the state of nature and "the state of reasoning" (which
is also necessarily a state of sociality).[21] For in this context, the

difference between legitimate government and despotism is simply irrelevant. All civilized men, whether they be citizens or slaves, are in a state of reasoning and of sociality.

There is no facile way to dispose of either of these two different concepts of the state of nature—both are manifestly present in the *Second Discourse*. In fact, the conflict between these two concepts of the state of nature may be seen as the root of the conflicting standards of praise and blame that inform the *Second Discourse* (and indeed Rousseau's thought as a whole). On the one hand, Rousseau praises the patriotic citizen (and Rome, Sparta, and Geneva) as opposed to the bourgeois (and the despotic regimes of eighteenth-century Europe) [22]; and on the other hand, he asserts the superiority of the way of life of savages over that of civilized men—*including* patriotic citizens.[23] The superiority of the savage way of life reflects the superiority of the natural to the conventional—the state of nature is preferable to the artificiality of civilized life. But from the juridical perspective, the state of nature is a defective state (the presence of legitimate government is clearly preferable to its absence), and the conventional therefore appears to be superior to the natural.

Fact and Right

The distinction between these two different perspectives may be further refined in the following manner: The state of nature understood as the state of animality reflects the point of view of "fact," while the state of nature understood as the absence of legitimate government reflects the point of view of "right" (*droit*). As he indicates in the last paragraph of the First Part, Rousseau regards man's original condition as he has portrayed it as a "fact."[24] (Similarly, the inequality that exists in the society of his time is a fact, whether that inequality be legitimate or not.) In this sense, the state of nature understood as man's original condition is *historical*, for history is the study of the facts of the development of the human race.[25] But facts are also the subject matter of science. And as has been pointed out before, the study of man's original condition is viewed by Rousseau as primarily a scientific inquiry, to be approached from the standpoint of physics.[26] Thus in Note L of the *Second Discourse* he makes the following remark in criticism of Locke's argument for the naturalness of the family:

> I shall observe first that moral proofs do not have great force in matters of physics, and that they serve rather to give a reason for existing facts than to prove the real existence of those facts. Such is the kind of proof Mr. Locke uses in the passage I have just quoted; for although it may be advantageous to the human species for the union between man and woman to be permanent, it does not follow that it was thus established by nature; otherwise it would be necessary to say that nature also instituted civil society, the arts, commerce, and all that is claimed to be useful to men.[27]

On the plane of fact—that is, in inquiries of a physical or strictly historical character—moral considerations have no place.

But if this is the case, Rousseau's account of the origin of *political* society cannot be strictly historical. This is first indicated in the Preface where he states: "The political and moral researches occasioned by the important question I examine are therefore useful in all ways; and the *hypothetical* history of governments is an instructive lesson for man in all respects."[28] It is Rousseau's account of the origin of political society—as distinguished from his account of man's original condition (and the factors that brought about his departure from that condition)—that is genuinely meant to be purely hypothetical. For it is not undertaken on the plane of fact proper to scientific or historical research; rather it belongs to the realm of "political and moral researches" which are undertaken from the standpoint of "right."

The strongest evidence for the nonhistorical or nonfactual

character of Rousseau's account of the beginnings of political society is his all but total neglect of any actual historical examples. (It is instructive to compare Rousseau's silence on this matter with Locke's explicit consideration of the historical record in the *Second Treatise.*[29]) In his history of the human race, Rousseau places the establishment of political society only *after* the establishment of landed property. In other words, he totally ignores the obvious factual evidence that all preagricultural peoples who have been observed exhibit some form of political authority and subordination.

After proposing his own version of the origin of political society (a contract proposed by the rich but agreed to by all), Rousseau says, "Such was, *or ought to have been (dut être)* the origin of society and of laws. . . ."[30] He recognizes that many have attributed other origins to political society, but states that "the choice among these causes is indifferent to that which I wish to establish."[31] He rejects the possibility that political society was formed at the initiative of the poor because "it is reasonable to believe that a thing was invented by those to whom it is *useful* rather than by those whom it wrongs."[32] Similarly, he rejects the "hypothesis" that political society was established by conquest because "the right of conquest, as it is not a right, could not have founded any other. . . ."[33] Finally, after arguing that governments have not begun by arbitrary power, he adds that "*even if they had begun thus*, this power being by its nature illegitimate, could not have served as a foundation for the rights of society, nor consequently, for instituted inequality."[34]

It is clear, then, that in his discussion of the beginnings of political society, Rousseau relies upon the very kind of "moral proofs" (i.e., considerations of the just and the useful) that he refuses to admit in his discussion of man's original condition. This procedure is justified because, as is explicitly stated in the *Social Contract*, the body politic itself is a "*moral* body" (*corps moral*).[35] A political society that is illegitimate, and thus has no basis in right, is not truly a political society at all. Therefore, Rousseau is less concerned with the *origin* of government than with its *foundations*, that is, that which gives it a basis in right. Accordingly, he can characterize his procedure in the Second Part of the *Second Discourse* as one of "test[ing] the facts by right."[36] Similarly, in the *Social Contract* he criticizes Grotius for following precisely the opposite procedure: "His [Grotius's] most constant manner of reasoning is always to establish the right by the fact. One could employ a more consequent method, but not one more favorable to tyrants."[37] In the first (unpublished) version of the *Social Contract*, Rousseau offers an elaboration of this criticism that perfectly defines what has been termed here as the standpoint of right: "It is not a question of that which is, but of that which is suitable (*convenable*) and just, nor of power which one is forced to obey, but of power one is obliged to recognize."[38]

Natural Law

Now that it has been shown that the teaching of the *Second Discourse* moves sometimes on the plane of fact and sometimes on the plane of right, it is necessary to confront the problem of how these two aspects of Rousseau's thought are linked together. One may say that for Rousseau's predecessors and contemporaries, the typical way of bridging this gap between fact or nature on the one hand, and right or law on the other, is some form of the doctrine of natural law. The positive (i.e., conventional) laws of political societies have a basis in right if they are in harmony with the laws of nature. Such an understanding of the relation between fact and right is embodied in the question—posed by the Academy of Dijon—to which the *Second Discourse* is addressed: "What is the origin of inequality among men, and is it authorized by natural law?" But as many commentators have noted, the title that Rousseau gives to his own essay indicates that he believed this question to have been badly formulated.[39] By entitling his work a *Discourse on the Origin and Foundations of Inequality Among Men*, Rousseau replaces the question of whether equality is authorized by natural law with the broader question of what are the foundations of inequality. He thereby implies that the foundations of inequality and therefore of political society may be sought elsewhere than in the doctrine of natural law.

This suggestion is supported by Rousseau's criticism in the Preface of the natural law teachings of all previous authors. This criticism focuses upon two broad groups of natural law theorists: the "Roman jurists" and the "moderns." The natural law doctrine of the Roman jurists is based on their understanding of law as "the expression of the general relations established by nature among all animate beings for their common preservation"; because they regarded natural law as a rule which was imposed rather than prescribed, the Roman jurists subjected animals as well as men to this law.[40] In contrast, the moderns recognized as law only a "rule prescribed to a moral being—that is to say, intelligent, free, and considered in his relations with other beings"; therefore they limited the application of natural law to man, "the sole animal endowed with reason."[41] In terms of the opposition outlined earlier between the realm of physics and of fact on the one hand, and the realm of morality and of right on the other, the natural law of the Roman jurists belongs to the first realm and that of the moderns to the second. (This is not to say that either of these natural law doctrines *in its own terms* assumed a rigorous opposition between these two realms.)

After having indicated his dissatisfaction with all previous definitions of natural law, Rousseau stops short of offering a definition of his own. But he does state what he regards as the essential preconditions of natural law: "All that we can see very clearly about this law [i.e., natural law] is that, *for it to be law*, not only must the will of him who is bound by it be able to submit to it with knowledge; but also, *for it to be natural*, it must speak directly by nature's voice."[42] From this statement it is apparent, first of all, that Rousseau accepts the moderns' conception of law. Natural law may properly be considered *law* only if those who are subject to its dictates comply with them knowingly (i.e., freely). Law must belong to the realm of morality rather than the realm of physics.

But if Rousseau accepts the moderns' understanding of law, he rejects their understanding of nature. Thus he criticizes all modern definitions of natural law for being derived from "knowledge which men do not naturally have."[43] As has been seen, a central tenet of the teaching of the *Second Discourse* is that reason is not natural to man, but is something that is acquired only after men have left the (primitive) state of nature. It is on this account that Rousseau asserts that to be natural, the law of nature "must speak directly by nature's voice" —that is, it must speak to man not by way of his reason, but by way of his passions. To be natural, the law of nature must be based upon "principles anterior to reason," or upon "interior impulsion" (*l'impulsion intérieure*).[44]

It should by now have become clear that the two criteria which Rousseau asserts must be met by a proper definition of natural law are mutually exclusive. And this is because, according to Rousseau, nature and law are mutually exclusive (the one belongs to the realm of physics, and the other to the realm of morality). Law can speak only to a being that possesses intelligence and moral liberty. But *by nature* man does not possess intelligence and moral liberty. Therefore nature cannot speak to man's reason, but only to the passions which he shares with the lower animals. Nature can only impose; it cannot prescribe. In short, according to Rousseau's own criteria, properly speaking *there can be no natural law*.

The same conclusion can be reached by a related but slightly different line of argument. Rousseau agrees with the moderns that anything that may properly be called law must be submitted to with knowledge. Therefore, he also agrees with the moderns that animals cannot be subject to natural law: "[F]or it is clear that, being devoid of intellect and of freedom, they cannot recognize this law."[45] But according to Rousseau, men also are by nature devoid of reason, and therefore man is fundamentally an animal like any other. Hence man cannot be subjected to natural law any more than are the other animals —and thus there can be no natural law.

It is true, of course, that as a result of the historical process outlined in the *Second Discourse*, men eventually do become reasoning beings, capable of knowingly complying with a prescriptive moral law. But how could any such law be considered natural if it has no application to man in his natural state, especially since man's department from that state is in no way foreordained, but is the product of accidents that might never have happened? Man becomes a moral and rational being by chance and not by nature. Therefore, no moral law or "law or reason" can be a law of nature.[46]

The Transition to Political Society

If law does not have its origin or its foundations in nature, it must be created by men. There must then be a "moment" in human history when for the first time "nature was subjected to law."[47] This moment coincides with the founding of political society: "This passage from the state of nature to the civil state produces in man a most remarkable change, substituting in his conduct justice for instinct, and giving to his actions the morality which was lacking in them before."[48] In establishing the laws of political society, men thereby create the foundations of morality and justice. "For law is anterior to justice, and not justice to law."[49]

Now in one sense this priority of political laws to justice

can be found in Hobbes's doctrine as well. Hobbes asserts, "Where there is no common power, there is no law; where no law, no injustice."[50] Yet at the center of Hobbes's political teaching there lies a doctrine of natural law, which serves as a link between the state of nature and civil society. It is true that Hobbes holds that the laws of nature are not really *laws* in the precise sense, and would more properly be designated "dictates of reason"; for "law, properly, is the word of him that by right hath command over others."[51] To become effective, or to become properly law, the "laws of nature" must be supplemented by sanctions imposed by men—that is, they must be embodied in positive law, the enactments of the soverign power of a civil society.

Yet for Hobbes the *content* of natural law is determined independently of the enactment of positive laws. Therefore, Hobbes can say, "The laws of nature are immutable and eternal, for injustice, ingratitude, arrogance, pride, iniquity, acception of persons and the rest can never be made lawful."[52] Similarly, he holds that if the laws of nature do not oblige men *in effect* (*in foro externo*) in the state of nature, they nevertheless always oblige men *in conscience* (*in foro interno*)—"that is to say, they bind to a desire they should take place."[53] Even if it is not always effective, the law of nature does speak to men in the state of nature. In particular, the law of nature bids men who are in a state of nature to seek to form a civil society.[54]

This last is the crucial point. According to Hobbes, the natural condition of men is always and everywhere a state of war. Hence, given the nature of men, whose greatest passion is the desire for their own self-preservation, their natural condition is always and everywhere a condition of misery. Thus the very fact of their natural condition bids men to seek to alter that condition by putting an end to the state of war through the establishment of civil society. In one sense, by seeking to alter their natural condition, men may be said to act *against* nature. But such action against nature is at the same time prompted by the nature of man itself.

The miserable and unstable character of the Hobbesian state of nature is constituted by this contradiction between man's nature and the condition in which he is placed by nature. Man's passions (above all, the fear of death) compel him to attempt to eliminate this contradiction. But it is man's reason that makes its elimination possible by suggesting the "articles of peace" that serve as the foundation of civil society.[55] In his political teaching at least, Hobbes, unlike Rousseau, accepts reason as an essential part of man's nature. Therefore the "conclusions, or theorems"[56] of reason on the basis of which men abolish the state of nature can also be considered natural. Man's eternal and unchanging nature determines the direction in which man transforms his natural condition, and thus serves as a link between the realm of fact and the realm of right.

For Rousseau, by contrast, the gap between these two realms must be much wider, since man's nature is itself viewed as changeable. The passage from the Rousseauan state of nature to political society involves not just a transformation of man's natural condition, but also and more importantly, a transformation of human nature. This transformation of human nature may be considered as having two stages. In the first place, there is the accidental process by which the stupid and self-sufficient animal of the primitive state of nature is transformed into a being possessing both reason and a host of artificial passions that make him dependent upon the assistance of his fellowmen. Through this process, one may say, the man of Rousseau's original state of nature becomes a being all but indistinguishable from the war-prone man of the Hobbesian state of nature.[57] But for this war-prone man to become a genuine citizen of political society, a further transformation (or "socialization") of human nature must take place. Rousseau presents his most complete statement of what this involves in his chapter on "The Legislator" in the *Social Contract*:

He who would undertake to legislate for a people must feel himself capable of changing, so to speak, human nature; of transforming each individual, who by himself is a perfect and solitary whole, into a part of a greater whole from which this individual receives in some manner his life and his being; of altering the constitution of man in order to reinforce it; of substituting a partial and moral existence for the physical and independent existence that we have all received from nature.[58]

The essence of this further transformation is succinctly stated in a sentence from the *Emile*: "Good social institutions are those that are best able to *denature* man."[59] The establishment of political society does not mean altering man's natural condition to bring it into harmony with his nature; it means changing man's nature—"denaturing" man—to bring him into harmony with the unnatural social condition at which he has accidentally arrived.

Self-preservation and Happiness

Every stage of the analysis of Rousseau's teaching up to this point has served only to emphasize the immense gap that exists between nature and political society, between the realm of fact and the realm of right. It is now time to seek out those elements of Rousseau's thought that might serve to bridge this gap, and to consider if even the denaturing of man required by a good political society does not in some positive sense take its bearings by standards derived from nature. The first and most obvious link between nature and political society in the thought of Rousseau is the goal of self-preservation. The desire for self-preservation is by nature the chief principle of man's conduct.[60] It is the concern for their self-preservation that prompts men living in the warlike conditions of the last stage of the state of nature to agree to the establishment of political society.[61] The pact which forms the body politic, Rousseau says in the *Social Contract*, "has for its end the preservation of the contractors."[62]

In recognizing self-preservation as the end of civil society, Rousseau clearly puts himself in agreement with Hobbes. But it is equally clear that Rousseau disagrees with Hobbes as to what constitutes a legitimate political society. In the first place, this is because Rousseau follows Locke in holding that the submission to arbitrary power is even less conducive to men's self-preservation than is the absence of any common power.[63] From the point of view of self-preservation, even civil war may be preferable to living under tyranny. Yet Rousseau's critique of Hobbes regarding what constitutes a legitimate political society manifestly goes beyond their disagreement over the most effective means of insuring self-preservation. For the whole thrust of Rousseau's attack on "civilized" society in both the *First Discourse* and the *Second Discourse* is directed especially against the kind of society favored by Hobbes and Locke, a society characterized by the flourishing of the arts, industry, commerce, and luxury. For Rousseau, the great vice of such a society is that it renders men dependent on one another without giving them a true community of interests. It makes them economic and social rivals first, and fellow citizens only secondarily. A member of such a society is dependent on the goodwill of others, yet always seeking to get the better of others:

> Always in contradiction with himself, always floating between his desires and his duties, he will never be either man or citizen; he will be good neither for himself nor for others. This will be one of the men of our age; a Frenchman, an Englishman, a bourgeois; this will be nothing.[64]

The political solution of Hobbes, or what may be called the bourgeois solution, does not really solve the problem of men living in the state of war (according to Rousseau, of course, this is not the true state of nature, but only the last stage of the state of nature). For Rousseau sees this problem not merely as a conflict between the state of war and the desire for self-pres-ervation, but also as a conflict between man's selfish passions and his dependence on others. The Hobbesian solution may remove the first contradiction, but it only deepens the second. It may make men more secure, but it also makes them miserable. Man's happiness demands more than just his security. Only to the extent that the contradiction between man's duties and his desires can be eliminated will the state of civil society cease to be a state of misery.

Now this contradiction between desires and duties, be-tween selfishness and the requirements of social life, is, of course, absent in the true state of nature, where man has no duties and is not at all dependent. In the true state of nature, man is happy because he is in harmony with himself; he is able to satisfy all his desires through his own efforts, and therefore he is always able to follow his own inclinations. Man is happy in the true state of nature because he is wholly self-sufficient and therefore totally independent. Man's happiness is identical with his freedom.

Freedom

If political society is to be compatible with human hap-piness, it must, then, provide not merely for men's security but also for their freedom. Consequently, Rousseau states the political problem in the following terms:

> To find a form of association that defends and protects with the whole force of the community the person and the goods of each associate, and by which each one uniting himself to all nevertheless obeys only himself and *remains as free as before*.[65]

The association that forms political society must preserve to the greatest extent possible the freedom that characterizes the state of nature. But men living in political society cannot possibly enjoy the self-sufficiency and total independence that they possess in the state of nature since their lives must be essentially bound up with their relations with their fellow citizens. Hence the citizen cannot possibly partake of the complete freedom to follow his inclinations that primitive man enjoys. He must instead exchange his "natural freedom" for "civil freedom," which is not merely compatible with but demands obedience to the laws.[66] Here, once again, it is instructive to compare Rousseau's teaching with that of Hobbes. For Hobbes, liberty is simply inconsistent with law or with any obligation whatsoever. Hence, in entering civil society and consenting to submit to its laws, men necessarily suffer a restriction of their liberty.[67] This is equally true for Rousseau insofar as "natural freedom" is concerned; but in his notion of "civil freedom," Rousseau asserts the existence of a kind of liberty the very essence of which consists in obedience to law.

The question of the relation between nature and law in the thought of Rousseau may then be posed in these terms: What is the connection between Rousseau's concept of natural freedom and his concept of civil freedom? First of all, one may say that civil freedom, like natural freedom, consists in independence of the wills of other men. By leaving the state of war, where he could be constrained to obey the will of an individual stronger than himself, and entering political society, a man brings himself closer to the freedom enjoyed by men in the true state of nature. Because he submits himself completely to the laws of a political society, the citizen is free of all "personal dependence."[68]

This aspect of civil freedom is unrelated to the source from which the laws of political society originate. The rule of laws would equally well eliminate "personal dependence" if the laws were imposed upon men by a superior being or by nature.[69] But the same does not hold true for another aspect of civil freedom: Each citizen of a properly constructed political society, according to Rousseau, is free also because he has an equal share in making the laws of that society; therefore, in obeying those laws, he is in a sense obeying himself. Civil freedom consists in participation in and obedience to the general will.[70]

The doctrine of the general will constitutes the most complex and controversial aspect of the fully developed political teaching that Rousseau presents in the *Social Contract*. In the present context, however, the essential point regarding this doctrine is that the general will, which is the source of the laws and hence of justice, has no foundation outside the wills of the citizens.[71] The general will does not exist by nature, since human society does not exist by nature. The general will and the laws that it pronounces are therefore produced by the art of men. The citizens are free because they not only approve the laws that they must obey, they themselves create those laws.

In the true state of nature, man is subject to no laws, not even to natural law. In this sense his freedom is unlimited and much greater even than the freedom that Hobbes attributed to man in the state of nature. He can give himself any law that he chooses. So long as man remains in the stupid animality of the state of nature, where his conduct is governed solely by instinct, this kind of freedom is, of course, meaningless. But when the accidental process described in the *Second Discourse* has transformed man into a reasonable and sociable being and compelled him to enter political society, he can gain real freedom to create the laws he chooses and thus to determine the conditions under which he lives with his fellowmen.[72] As long as each citizen partakes on an equal basis in the creation of such laws, all equally enjoy this freedom.

This civil freedom involves a restriction of the natural freedom to follow one's own private will whenever that private will is in conflict with the general will. Therefore, men enjoy the greatest possible combination of civil freedom and natural freedom when their private wills are most in accord with the general will. Man is most free when he is most fully socialized —that is, when he has most fully transformed or "denatured" himself.

Divine Will and Human Art

Because the transformation of man from a stupid animal to a moral being and a citizen represents for Rousseau the denaturing of man, he views political society as being even more artificial than Hobbes had viewed it. In a sense, man's humanity itself must be understood as the product of human art. It is true that man's departure from his original, bestial condition and his progress beyond it are the result of accidents. But the dynamics of this progress depend upon the reactions of men to the accidents that befall them and the new circumstances in which they find themselves—reactions that are not wholly determined by nature. To take perhaps the most important example, language, the essential condition of man's humanity, is an invention, a product of human art developed in response to evolving circumstances.[73] Therefore, by the time he arrives at the stage of historical development at which he both has need of and is capable of political society, man is already very much the product of art. While for Hobbes the establishment of political society represents art correcting nature, for Rousseau it represents art correcting art.

The question of the role of human art in the establishment of political society is broached in the Preface of the *Second Discourse*:

Now without serious study of man, of his natural faculties and their successive developments, one will never succeed in

[*115*]

making such distinctions and in separating, in the present constitution of things, what divine will has done from what *human art* has pretended to do. The political and moral researches occasioned by the important question I examine are therefore useful in all ways; and the hypothetical history of governments is an instructive lesson for man in all respects. By considering what we would have become abandoned to ourselves, we ought to learn to bless him whose beneficent hand, correcting our institutions and giving them an unshakeable base, has prevented the disorders which must otherwise have resulted from them, and has created our happiness from the means that seemed likely to heighten our misery.

> *Quem te Deus esse*
> *Jussit, et humana qua parte locatus es in re,*
> *Disce.*[74]

In opposing the claim of human art to that of divine will, Rousseau in this passage appears to suggest that only the latter is capable of correcting the abuses of political society and giving it solid foundations. This suggestion is seemingly confirmed in the Second Part of the *Discourse* where Rousseau speaks of "how much human governments needed a basis more solid than reason alone, and how necessary it was for public repose that divine will intervened to give sovereign authority a sacred and inviolable character. . . ."[75] Yet this invocation of divine will as the true basis of political society and thereby of human happiness hardly seems credible in the light of the rest of the *Second Discourse* or of Rousseau's political writings as a whole.[76] In the chapter on "The Legislator" in the *Social Contract*, Rousseau presents a much fuller and more open account of his views on the role of religion in the foundation of the state. It is the shortsightedness of "the people" that "forced in all times the fathers of nations to have recourse to the intervention of heaven and to honor the gods with their own wisdom."⁷⁷ The legislator "puts his decisions in the mouths of immortals to persuade by divine authority those who could not be moved by human prudence."⁷⁸ What Rousseau refers to in the *Second Discourse* as "divine will" thus turns out itself to be a product of human art.

This conclusion emerges still more clearly from chapter two of the first version of the *Social Contract*. In this chapter Rousseau searches for a "solid" response to the arguments of a man who "lives at the same time in the liberty of the state of nature and subjected to the needs of the social state" and who prefers to maintain his full independence—even if this puts him in a state of war with other men—rather than to submit to any obligations whatever.⁷⁹ Here "the will of God" is explicitly rejected as an adequate response; similarly found wanting are the law of nature, the "general will of the human race," and "the interior voice" or conscience.⁸⁰ Having rejected these alternatives, Rousseau continues as follows:

> Far from thinking that there is neither virtue nor happiness for us, and *that heaven has abandoned us* without resource to the depravation of the species, let us force ourselves to draw from the evil itself the remedy which should cure us. By new associations, let us correct, if possible, the absence of the general association [i.e., a general society of the human race]. Let our violent interlocutor himself judge of our success. Let us show him in *art perfected (l'art perfectionné) the reparation of the evils that unperfected art (l'art commencé) did to nature*: Let us show him all the misery of the state he believes happy, all the error of the reasoning that he believes solid. Let him see in a better constitution of things the reward of good actions, the chastisement of bad actions, and the pleasing accord of justice and happiness. Let us enlighten his reason with new lights, warm his heart with new sentiments, and teach him to multiply his being and his felicity in sharing them with his fellowmen.⁸¹

If the passage from the Preface of the *Second Discourse* quoted earlier is reconsidered in the light of this one, some striking conclusions emerge. Men have indeed been "abandoned to themselves" by heaven, but this does not mean that they are "without resource." Divine will does not "correct our institutions" and it has not "created our happiness." But human art is capable of accomplishing what divine will has failed to do. By establishing a properly organized political society, man can repair the evils that were occasioned by his accidental departure from the original state of nature.

As the *Second Discourse* makes clear, however, this does not mean that all or perhaps any existing civil societies have accomplished this task. The art of most founders of civil societies was far from "perfected":

Nascent government did not have a constant and regular form. The lack of philosophy and experience allowed only present inconveniences to be perceived, and men thought of remedying others only as they presented themselves. Despite all the labors of the wisest legislators, the political state remained ever imperfect because it was almost the work of chance, and because, as it began badly, time in discovering faults and suggesting remedies could never repair the vices of the constitution. People incessantly mended, whereas it would have been necessary to begin by clearing the area and setting aside all the old materials, as Lycurgus did in Sparta, in order to raise a good edifice afterward.[82]

Political societies were radically imperfect in their origins because of a "lack of philosophy and experience." But in the Preface Rousseau indicates that this lack persists in his own time: "the true foundations of the body politic" remain misunderstood.[83] By laying bare those "true foundations," by setting forth "the principles of political right," Rousseau makes possible for the first time the perfection of the legislative art, or the possibility of establishing a political society that will no longer be "almost the work of chance." It may not be too far-fetched to suggest that Rousseau in some measure regards *himself* as the being "whose beneficent hand" has shown us humans how we can create "our happiness from the means which seemed likely to crown our misery."

The Invincibility of Nature

Yet however grandiose Rousseau's conception of his own role as a teacher of legislators may have been, it did not blind him to the limits of what can be accomplished by human beings. For no matter how potent the art of the legislator may be, Rousseau understood that it could never succeed in wholly transforming a physical being into a moral being—that is, in completely denaturing man:

> The difference between human art and the work of nature makes itself felt in its effects; the citizens may call themselves members of the state, but they are not able to unite themselves to it as true members are united to the body. It is impossible to achieve that each of them not have an individual and separate existence, by which he alone is able to suffice to his own preservation.[84]

Indeed, in the final analysis, all of man's labors to establish a realm of morality and of right are incapable of altering the underlying nature of things at all.

> At bottom, the body politic, being nothing more than a moral person, is nothing more than a being of reason. Take away the public convention, and instantly the state is destroyed without the least alteration in all that composes it; and all the conventions of men will never be able to change anything in the nature (*physique*) of things.[85]

The two striking passages quoted above are taken from a fragmentary writing of Rousseau on the state of war, but the point of view they express is present even in the *Social Con-*

tract. "A perfect legislation" demands that the general will always predominate over particular wills. But "according to the natural order," the particular will is always stronger than the general will.[86] Civil freedom can never be made wholly compatible with natural freedom. Therefore men living in political society are always "in chains."[87] The freedom and happiness of natural man can never be attained by the citizen, for in the last analysis man will always remain a "physical" being, and thus a "perfect and solitary whole."[88]

The individualist emphasis of the *Second Discourse*, then, reflects the deepest level of Rousseau's thought more adequately than does the collectivist emphasis of the *Social Contract* or the *First Discourse*. Nature remains ultimately superior to convention. And from the strict standpoint of nature, the life of the citizen is no less inadequate than that of the bourgeois. The citizen as well as the bourgeois lives outside himself. He seeks his happiness in the judgments of others (i.e., his fellow citizens).[89] But since man, no matter how collectivized, always must remain at bottom a solitary individual, his happiness can only be found in himself. Even the best political society, then, is unable fully to solve the problem that was posed for man by his accidental departure from his original animal condition. Full citizenship in a good political society is merely the best that can be done for the great mass of men to minimize the evils of the unnatural condition to which they have been condemned by history. Whether a more satisfactory solution can be found for a few individuals who live in society is a question of a very different kind, one that has little bearing on "the true foundations of the body politic" or "the principles of political right." For Rousseau's judgment on this matter, one would have to turn to the *Emile*, the *Confessions*, and the *Reveries of a Solitary Walker*.

Notes

[1] See above, pp. 11–14.

[2] *Second Discourse*, p. 96 [P, 3:126].

[3] *Contract social*, 1, chap. 4 [P, 3:355].

[4] Diderot, *Oeuvres politiques*, ed. P. Vernière (Paris: Garnier, 1963), p. 9.

[5] Thomas Hobbes, *Leviathan*, ed., Michael Oakeshott (Oxford: Basil Blackwell, 1960), 1, chap. 13, p. 80; John Locke, *Second Treatise*, 2, sec. 4; 4, sec. 22.

[6] Diderot, *Oeuvres politiques*, ed. P. Vernière, p. 6.

[7] *Second Discourse*, pp. 97, 103, 170, 180 [P, 3:127, 133, 185–86, 193].

[8] Ibid., pp. 161–62, 165–66, 168, 177–78 [P, 3:179, 182, 184, 191]; *Contract social*, 1, chaps. 2–3 [P, 3:352–55].

[9] Aristotle, *Politics*, 1254a18–1255a3.

[10] Cf. *Contract social*, 1, chap. 2 [P, 3:353].

[11] Ibid., 1, chap. 2 [P, 3:352].

[12] *Second Discourse*, pp. 177–78 [P, 3:191].

[13] Ibid., p. 177 [P, 3:191].

[14] Ibid., pp. 163–68 [P, 3:180–84]; Locke, *Second Treatise*, 4, sec. 23; 15, sec. 172.

[15] *Second Discourse*, p. 142 [P, 3:164].

[16] Ibid., p. 150; Note J, p. 204 [P, 3:170, 208] (italics mine).

[17] Ibid., p. 102 [P, 3:132].

[18] See above, pp. 17–25, 34–38, 51, 70–73.

¹⁹ *Second Discourse*, pp. 121, 138, 150; Note L, p. 217; Note O, p. 222 [P, 3:147, 160, 170, 216, 217, 219] (italics mine).

²⁰ Ibid., Note L, p. 219 [P, 3:217].

²¹ Ibid., p. 132 [P, 3:155–56].

²² Ibid., pp. 78–90, 171, 178 [P, 3:111–21, 186, 192].

²³ Ibid., pp. 161, 178–80; Note I, pp. 192–203 [P, 3:179, 192–93, 202–8].

²⁴ Ibid., p. 141 [P, 3:162].

²⁵ Ibid., p. 141 [P, 3:163]; *Emile*, P, 4:527–28.

²⁶ See above, pp. 22–23.

²⁷ *Second Discourse*, Note L, pp. 215–16 [P, 3:215–16].

²⁸ Ibid., p. 97 [P, 3:127] (italics mine).

²⁹ Locke, *Second Treatise*, 8 ("Of the Beginning of Political Societies").

³⁰ *Second Discourse*, p. 160 [P, 3:178] (italics mine).

³¹ Ibid., p. 161 [P, 3:179].

³² Ibid., p. 162 [P, 3:180] (italics mine).

³³ Ibid., p. 161 [P, 3:179].

³⁴ Ibid., p. 168 [P, 3:184] (italics mine).

³⁵ *Contract social*, 1, chap. 6 [P, 3:361] (italics mine). Rousseau also calls the state a *personne morale*: Ibid., 1, chap. 7; 2, chap. 4 [P, 3:363, 372].

³⁶ *Second Discourse*, p. 166 [P, 3:182].

³⁷ *Contract social*, 1, chap. 2 [P, 3:353].

³⁸ *Contract social (première version)*, 1, chap. 5 [P, 3:305]. Consider also the following passage at the beginning of this chapter [P, 3:297]: "Il y a mille maniéres de rassembler les hommes, il n'y en a qu'une de les unir. C'est pour cela que je ne donne dans cet ouvrage qu'une méthode pour la formation des sociétés politiques quoique dans la multitude d'aggrégations qui éxistent actuel-

lement sous ce nom, il n'y en ait peut être pas deux qui aient été formées de la même maniére, et pas une qui l'ait été selon celle que j'établis. *Mais je cherche le droit et la raison et ne dispute pas des faits*" (italics mine).

39 *Second Discourse*, P, 3:125 (note 2); Robert Derathé, *Jean-Jacques Rousseau et la science politique de son temps* (Paris: Presses Universitaires de France, 1950) p. 156; Pierre Burgelin, *La Philosophie de l'existence de J-J Rousseau* (Paris: Presses Universitaires de France, 1952), p. 509.

40 *Second Discourse*, p. 94 [P, 3:124].

41 Ibid., p. 94 [P, 3:124].

42 Ibid., p. 95 [P, 3:125] (italics mine).

43 Ibid., p. 95 [P, 3:125].

44 Ibid., pp. 95–96 [P, 3:125–26].

45 Ibid., p. 96 [P, 3:126].

46 Cf. *Contract social (première version)*, 1, chap. 2 [P, 3:284].

47 *Second Discourse*, p. 102 [P, 3:132].

48 *Contract social*, 1, chap. 8 [P, 3:364].

49 *Contract social (première version)*, 2, chap. 4 [P, 3:329].

50 Hobbes, *Leviathan*, 1, chap. 13, p. 83.

51 Ibid., 1, chap. 15, pp. 104–5.

52 Ibid., 1, chap. 14, p. 104; consider also Ibid., 2, chap. 26, p. 186: "Another division of laws, is into *natural* and *positive*. *Natural* are those which have been laws from all eternity. . . ." (italics in original).

53 Ibid., 1, chap. 15, p. 103.

54 Consider Hobbes's first two laws of nature. Ibid., 1, chap. 14, p. 85.

55 Ibid., 1, chap. 13, p. 84.

56 Ibid., 1, chap. 15, p. 104.

57 *Second Discourse*, p. 157 [P, 3:176].

⁵⁸ *Contract social*, 2, chap. 7 [P, 3:381].

⁵⁹ *Emile*, P, 4:249 (italics mine).

⁶⁰ *Second Discourse*, pp. 95–96, 142; Note O, p. 222 [P, 3:126, 164, 219]; *Contract social*, 1, chap. 2 [P, 3:352].

⁶¹ *Second Discourse*, pp. 157–60 [P, 3:176–78]; *Contract social*, 1, chap. 6 [P, 3:360].

⁶² *Contract social*, 2, chap. 5 [P, 3:376].

⁶³ *Second Discourse*, pp. 163–64 [P, 3:180–81]; Locke, *Second Treatise*, 19, sec. 228.

⁶⁴ *Emile*, P, 4:249–50.

⁶⁵ *Contract social*, 1, chap. 6 [P, 3:360] (italics mine).

⁶⁶ *Second Discourse*, p. 160 [P, 3:178]; *Contract social*, 1, chap. 8 [P, 3:364–65].

⁶⁷ Hobbes, *Leviathan*, 1, chap. 14, pp. 84–86.

⁶⁸ *Contract social*, 1, chap. 7; 2, chaps. 4, 12 [P, 3:364, 375, 394].

⁶⁹ Cf. *Emile*, P, 4:311.

⁷⁰ *Contract social*, 2, chap. 4 [P, 3:373–75].

⁷¹ Ibid., 2, chap. 4 [P, 3:375].

⁷² Men who live in the social state but are not genuine citizens may be free to indulge their private desires to a considerable extent, but they are unable to determine the shape of their society. Thus they lack the freedom to make many of those decisions that influence their own lives. This freedom is available only to the citizen who "participates" in the fundamental decisions made by the political community. The kind of freedom that comes from political participation is at the heart of Rousseau's concept of civil freedom.

⁷³ See above, pp. 33–34, 38.

⁷⁴ *Second Discourse*, p. 97 [P, 3:127] (italics mine). The Latin verse with which this passage concludes is from Persius (*Satires*, 3, 71–73): "Learn what God has commanded you to be, and what role you have been given in human affairs."

⁷⁵ Ibid., p. 170 [P, 3:186].

Notes

76 See above, pp. 31–33.

77 *Contract social*, 2, chap. 7 [P, 3:383].

78 Ibid., 2, chap. 7 [P, 3:384].

79 *Contract social (première version)*, 1, chap. 2 [P, 3:284–89].

80 Ibid., 1, chap. 2 [P, 3:285–87].

81 Ibid., 1, chap. 2 [P, 3:288] (italics mine).

82 *Second Discourse*, p. 162–63 [P, 3:180].

83 Ibid., p. 96 [P, 3:126].

84 *L'Etat de guerre*, P, 3:606; Cf. *Contract social*, 2, chap. 4 [P, 3:372].

85 *L'Etat de guerre*, P, 3:608.

86 *Contract social*, 3, chap. 2 [P, 3:401].

87 Ibid., 1, chap. 1 [P, 3:351].

88 Ibid., 2, chap. 7 [P, 3:381].

89 *Second Discourse*, pp. 178–79 [P, 3:192–93].

6

Conclusion

THIS BRIEF CONCLUDING CHAPTER will seek to draw together the essential elements of the foregoing interpretation of Rousseau's teaching in order to answer the question with which this study of the state of nature began: What are the common premises that underlie both the individualist and the collectivist sides of Rousseau's thought—and perhaps much subsequent radical thought as well?

The fundamental principle of Rousseau's thought, as he affirmed in several places, is that man is naturally good, and that society has depraved him.[1] In the *Second Discourse* Rousseau claims to have "demonstrated" this proposition.[2] He does this by showing that the state of nature is a state of peace and happiness, and not, as Hobbes had asserted, a state of war and misery.

The Hobbesian view of human nature and human society (which is essentially the bourgeois view) may be briefly stated as follows: All men are governed by selfish passions, above all the desire for their self-preservation, and no man has a greater right to what is necessary for his own preservation than does any other man. Each man is the sole judge of the best means to his own preservation; therefore, all men are naturally free. But men's selfish passions put them into perpetual conflict with one another. It is in this sense that Hobbes's natural man is evil. The result is a condition of war, and hence of misery; for the object of men's strongest desire, self-preservation, is threatened by their very efforts to achieve it. Hobbes's remedy for the evils of this natural condition of mankind is a civil society that is built upon men's selfish passions, but seeks to channel them in such a way that the conflict that makes men miserable is eliminated. The function of government is to provide for men's peace, safety, and comfort, and thus to secure the preconditions of their individual pursuit of happiness.

Up to a certain point, Rousseau agrees with the Hobbesian analysis of human nature. He too regards natural man as a being who is essentially selfish and governed by the desire for his own preservation. And he also holds that every man is naturally free and his own master. But Rousseau disagrees with the Hobbesian appraisal of man's natural condition, not because he holds a *higher* view of human nature, but because he believes man's nature is even *lower* than Hobbes had thought. The state of nature is a state of peace not because men are naturally governed by natural law, or reason, or conscience, or even compassion; it is a state of peace because natural man is so primitive (i.e., stupid) that he has only the most rudimentary desires. And *these* desires are so easily satisfied that men are not forced into a situation of conflict with one another. It is in this sense that one must understand Rousseau's contention that nature has made man happy and good. Men in the state of nature are not mutual enemies perpetually at war with every other member of their species for the same reason that monkeys or wolves are not perpetually at war with every other member of their own species.

The basis for this Rousseauan view of the natural and original condition of mankind is not the Biblical story of the Garden of Eden, not some poetic myth of the "Golden Age," not a plumbing of the depths of his own personality, and not some purely hypothetical construct of what men would be like in an asocial condition. The primary source of the Rousseauan state of nature is evidence derived from the behavior of other species of animals. And the crucial premise that allows Rousseau to identify the natural condition of man with the animal condition lies in the understanding of nature and of man's place in nature supplied by modern physical science. The human species is not eternal, and it is not the product of a special act of divine creation; it came into being through the workings of those ordinary processes of mechanical causation by which, over long periods of time, more complex beings evolve from simpler ones. By nature, then, man may be a slightly more complex being than the other animals, but this difference is, so to speak, a quantitative rather than a qualitative one. *Nature* has placed no "specific distinction" between man and other living beings. In the decisive respects, man is by nature merely an animal like any other.

At some point, however, man rises above the purely animal-like situation in which he is placed by nature. Rousseau expresses that which enables man to rise above his primitive nature by the term "perfectibility." Yet perfectibility cannot be understood as a faculty inherent in man's nature that points to or intends his progress beyond an animal condition. It merely refers to whatever it is in man that allows for the *possibility* of his progress. The notion of potentiality contained in the Rousseauan concept of perfectibility is of a wholly nonteleological kind. For example, suppose that man's upright posture is the necessary condition of his development of reason, that which makes it *possible*. This does not mean, however, that man is endowed with upright posture *because* he is destined to become a reasoning being. Nor does it even mean that because man has upright posture it was necessary or inevitable that he become a reasoning being. Although upright posture may make man's acquisition of reason possible, it does not make that acquisition any the less accidental. Rousseau makes it quite clear that all of man's progress beyond his animal condition is the result of "accidents" that might never have happened.

These accidents, and men's responses to them, lead to the development of everything about man one usually thinks of as specifically human: language, reason, morality, culture, and society. None of these attributes of civilized human life are intended by nature; therefore, nature is absolved of responsibility for whatever evils they may bring in their train. It is in this sense that "man has hardly any evils other than those he has given himself, and that nature . . . [is] justified."[3]

As a consequence of the alterations in their constitutions produced by the accidental departure from their primitive condition, men eventually begin to form societies. But then men's constitutions are, in turn, further altered by the experience of living under social conditions. As they become sociable, their desires begin to be shaped by the opinions of those with whom they live; they become less concerned with the satisfaction of their own natural needs than with their superiority over other men. Yet at the same time that their natural selfishness is exacerbated in this way, men's freedom to follow their own desires must be curbed in accordance with the requirements of peace and self-preservation in a social setting. Therefore government becomes necessary, and men acquire the unnatural habits of ruling and obeying. In these ways men are formed—or deformed—by the society in which they live, and they become wicked, slavish, and miserable.

It is Rousseau's low view of human nature that leads him to attack civil society as such, in a way no previous political philosopher had ever done. From the perspective of classical political philosophy, civil society appeared as the essential ful-

Conclusion

fillment of man's rational and social nature. And from the perspective of Hobbes and his followers, civil society appeared as
the essential remedy for overcoming the evils of man's natural
condition: Government is necessary to channel man's natural
passions in such a way that they may be all the more efficiently
satisfied. But for Rousseau, the passions that render civil society
necessary are in no way natural to man. They are rather themselves the product of a series of accidents that transform man's
original nature and make him a social being. For Rousseau,
then, civil society is not an *essential* necessity for man, but
merely an *accidental* necessity at a certain stage in human history. As a result, the real value of civil society itself is radically
called into question.

This doubt about the essential worth and necessity of civil
society—which, to repeat, derives from Rousseau's low view
of human nature—gives rise to two responses, and lends to each
of them an extreme or radical character. The first and more
obvious response is the condemnation of all civil society (and
the artificiality and constraint that inevitably accompany it)
in the name of nature and of individual freedom. The implications of this position are simply anti-political. But the
Rousseauan premises outlined above may also lead to another
response, one that is emphatically political, and that leads not
to turning one's back on political society, but to the attempt
to perfect political society.

For if the character of social man is so little determined by
nature, and to so great an extent shaped by the society in which
he lives, then a reordering of civil society may bring about
changes of the greatest magnitude in the characters of its citizens. The artificiality of social man, and the distance that he
has already traveled beyond his original nature, indicate how
great a possibility there is of transforming him much further
still, and of giving a new shape to his humanity. Bourgeois society merely takes social man as he is, a member of society who

nevertheless is governed by his own selfish passions rather than the common good. Those who live in such a society, Rousseau argues, will always be torn between their selfish desires and their social duties, and hence will always be miserable. But a further transformation of men can go a long way toward removing this contradiction fatal to human happiness, by making men over into true citizens who will prefer the common good to their own private good—that is, by making them into genuinely social men.

The connection between Rousseau's view of natural man and his vision of a more perfect political order does not lie in any natural disposition of man (such as compassion) that points toward human society. It lies rather in the very primitiveness of man's nature, and the extraordinary degree to which it may therefore be altered by human art. Thus the collectivist side of Rousseau's thought, as well as the individualist side, is ultimately traceable back to the low or "primitive" view of human nature presented in the *Second Discourse*. And it is likely that a comparable view of human nature may be the half-forgotten premise of subsequent radical doctrines that attack an "oppressive" society in the name of both individual freedom and the vision of a true community. It may be doubted, however, that Rousseau's followers have ever displayed his clear and painful awareness of the ineradicable tension between these two points of view.

Notes

¹ *Second Discourse*, p. 193 [P, 3:202]; *Rousseau juge de Jean-Jacques*, P, 1:934; *Lettre à Beaumont*, P, 4:935.

² *Second Discourse*, p. 193 [P, 3:202].

³ Ibid., p. 193 [P, 3:202].

Index

Index

Index

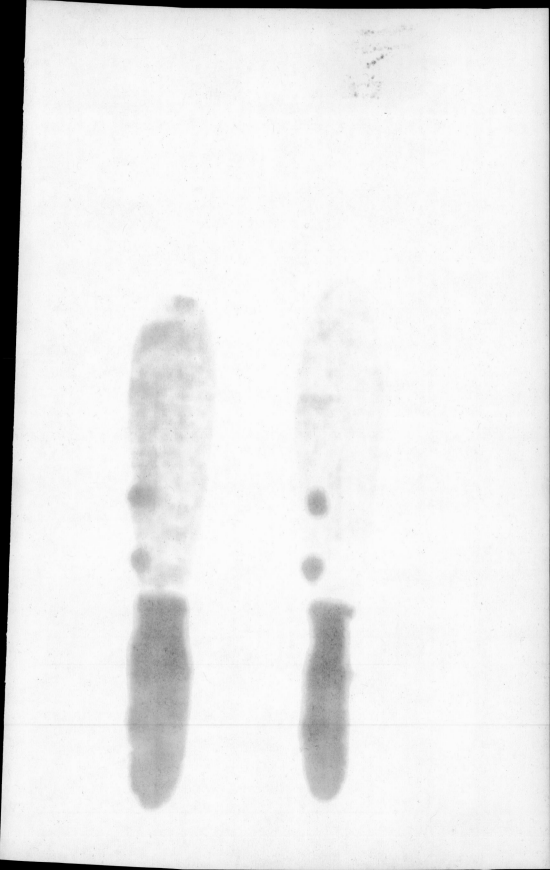